VOLUME II

Copyright © 1996

All rights reserved.
This book, or any part thereof,
may not be reproduced in any
form whatsoever without the express
written permission of the copyright holder.

Published and distributed
in the U.S. and overseas by:
C.I.S. Publishers and Distributors
180 Park Avenue, Lakewood, New Jersey 08701
(908) 905-3000 Fax: (908) 367-6666

Book and cover design: Deenee Cohen
Typography: Nechamie Miller

ISBN 1-56062-308-X hard cover
1-56062-309-8 soft cover

PRINTED IN THE UNITED STATES OF AMERICA

Visions of Greatness

VOLUME II

A COLLECTION OF INSPIRATIONAL STORIES

RABBI YOSEF WEISS

C.I.S. PUBLISHERS

New York • London • Jerusalem

הסכמת הרב שמואל קמנצקי שליט"א

ישיבה דפילאדעלפיא

בס"ד

יום ג לספר ומפרו של אברהם פב"ק

לכבוד הרב הגאון הצדיק והעניו לשד"ר
הגאון קראים וכו' ה'מו' ר' ... הלוי שליט"א

אחדשה"ט בעילוי הכוד להודות.

הביט על סיפורי אבותינו אשר עלו להן עולות
וקן דינים כעלותו דהלאן כי רב סיפור וכן סגולותיהן
למעוד. ועי' ברמב"ם בפ"ק מהל' ת"ת דגם ומעשה
גם מי שאין מיד כותב חסדי השי"ת והפלאות וגודל וכו'
המסגלים ונמצאים לכל ישראל מצדיני עולם ומולדת.
יעודה כדי להתנות מצדיקי ואנשי הדור וגמלות
הפעולות הקודש וטהור גמר מאמתחתו.

הדורש לחוקם
[signature]

הסכמת הרב מאיר הערשקאוויץ שליט"א

ב"ה

ישיבת בית בנימין
ע"ש ר' בנימין יהודה הלוי פרוונסקי ז"ל

Bais Binyomin
Talmudic Research Center
DEDICATED TO THE MEMORY OF
BENJAMIN PRUZANSKY ז"ל

Rabbi Simcha Schustal
Rabbi Meyer Hershkowitz
Roshei Hayeshiva

Rabbi Dovid Hersh Mayer
Dean

ONE HUNDRED THIRTY TWO PROSPECT STREET / STAMFORD, CONNECTICUT 06901 / (203) 325-4351

Table of Contents

Introduction 11
Dedication—For Heaven's Sake 15

BOOK ONE: ETHICAL CONDUCT
    To Live as a Jew 25

BOOK TWO: FAITH AND DIVINE PROVIDENCE
    Entebbe Alive 67
    Remember, it's Shabbos! 80
    Mitzvah Protection 84
    In the Numbers 90
    A Gift of Life 97
    Long-Deferred Appreciation 101
    A Blessing Come True 105
    Frostbite 107
    Journey to Health 109
    Care for My Children 116
    Catalyst for a Car 118
    Lost and Found 122
    Saved by the Enemy 124
    A Mother's Kerchief 126

BOOK THREE: FEELINGS AND CONCERNS
    Flight from Heaven 131
    Strictly Business 135
    A Healing Visit 137
    Lest Others Stumble 140
    Concern for Klal Yisrael 143
    Heavenly Reliance 145
    A Moment of Truth 146
    Long-Term Success 149
    Designated Livelihood 155
    Admonishment with Love 157
    Sagacious Rebuke 158

BOOK FOUR: NOBLE ATTRIBUTES
    A Pearl to Remember 163
    Marooned in Maine 170
    A Run for It 181
    Anything for a Mother 184
    Tzedakah Incognito 187

BOOK FIVE: WORDS OF OUR SAGES
    On the Right Foot 193
    A Mother's Concern 198
    V'imru Amein 202
    A Diamond of a Lesson 207
    Run, My Child 208
    A Favor Returned 210
    A Rebbe's Foresight 213
    The Right Doctor 216
    Speak Softly 217
    The Tenth Man 218

Glossary 223

Introduction

It is with deep gratitude and praise to Hashem that I present this second volume of *Visions of Greatness* to the reading public. *Baruch Hashem*, the first volume was well received, and it was the warm response and encouragement of many of its readers that inspired me to write the present edition.

In actuality, I myself have been greatly inspired in preparing this work, and I am hopeful that others, too, will benefit immensely from reading these true stories.

The acquisition of positive character traits is not merely an admirable goal. Rather, each and every person is commanded by the Torah to strive to this end and to use it as a focal point in his service of Hashem.

However, in this life-long discipline, it is important to keep in mind a lesson often cited by the Manchester *rosh yeshivah*, Harav Yehudah Zev Segal *zatzal*, regarding one's inner battles in *avodas Hashem*.

In *Ruach Chaim* (3:1), R' Chaim Volozhiner offers a parable about a king who commands his servant to climb up to a roof. Certainly the king does not expect the servant to leap from the ground to the roof. The servant will need a ladder. However, if the king notices the servant standing still on one of the rungs of the ladder, and not ascending to the roof, he will naturally demand to know why the servant is not fulfilling his command.

This ladder concept must be considered in our *avodas Hashem*. While a person must improve himself gradually, he must also refrain from standing motionless on his current spiritual level. Certainly, one is not expected to become a *tzaddik* overnight. But he *is* expected to continue to cautiously climb the rungs of the ladder.

Thus, one should not feel despair if he realizes that he has not yet achieved perfection. He should concentrate on continuing his climb, on perfecting one good character attribute after another, as he gradually ascends the ladder to success.

The Rambam writes in his explanation on *Avos* (1:17) that there are five categories of speech. One of these categories is called "Beloved Speech," meaning talk that Hashem loves to hear from His people. This type of speech includes speaking about positive attributes and relating stories which portray these character traits, as well as praising distinguished people and their virtues, to enable others to learn from their ways.

It is my hope that this volume will inspire its readers to absorb the lessons related therein. May we always be inspired to elevate ourselves in the service of Hashem. And may we thereby merit the arrival of Mashiach, may it be speedily in our days.

ACKNOWLEDGMENTS

With praise and thanksgiving to Hashem, I would like to take this opportunity to thank those people who made this second volume a reality.

The distinguished contributors of the stories alloted their precious time to this project, and shared their personal encounters with the reading public. While great effort was expended to ensure that the recording of the stories was as faithful as possible, the responsibility for any errors that may have slipped in is mine alone.

Credit for this volume is due to Mrs. E. Langer of Lakewood, N.J., and Mrs. P. Soloveitchik of Yerushalayim. Their skillful editing of this edition have brought the stories to perfection.

My appreciation to Rabbi Aaron Goldman for proofreading the stories and adding his invaluable thoughts and suggestions.

I extend great respect to Rabbi Zissel Ellinson and the entire C.I.S. staff for their professional presentation of this book.

I am indebted to Mr. Isaac Friedman of Philadelphia for his assistance in the publication of this book. I can truthfully say that while working with Mr. Friedman, I have learned many lessons in *middos* and *ahavas Yisrael*, which deserve a book of their own.

A debt of gratitude is due to Rabbi Binyomin Friedland and Rabbi Yosef Gelbwachs, *roshei yeshivah* of Mesivta Ohr Chodosh and Beis Midrash Ohr Hatalmud. Their love and concern for every *talmid* is a lesson for all. A special note of thanks for all the encouragement they have given me while working on this project.

I would like to once again express my heartfelt *hakoras hatov* to my parents, Mr. and Mrs. Eliezer Weiss, my brother, R' Shlomo, and my in-laws, Rabbi and Mrs. Chaim Yaakov Davis and family. Together they created the foundation which made these projects possible. May they all be blessed with long life and good health, and enjoy much *nachas* from their families.

My wife Tova always stands at my side in our efforts to serve Hashem. May we merit to raise our children to attain Torah, *chupah* and *maasim tovim*.

Yosef Y. Weiss
Shevat, 1996

This book is dedicated to
Mr. Isaac Friedman
of Philadelphia, Pennsylvania,
a man whose heart is
permeated with the love of Torah
and is totally devoted
to the sake of his people.

FOR HEAVEN'S SAKE

It was 1943. World War II was raging in Europe. Mr. Isaac Friedman found himself in Groszvardan, a city on the Rumanian border, working in a labor camp under the auspices of the government.

One day, Mr. Friedman was given a forty-eight hour furlough. He decided to travel to the city of Satmar to see the Bixader Rebbe. It was well known that the Satmar Rebbe himself would visit the Bixader Rebbe every *erev Yom Kippur* with a *kvittel*. Mr. Friedman felt that this would be the best place for him to go to get some desperately needed advice.

Mr. Friedman came before the *rebbe* and posed his question: Should he return to his labor camp when his furlough was up, or should he use the opportunity to make a run for it?

"Return to the camp," the *rebbe* advised him. "They will soon dismiss you and allow you to return home."

Mr. Friedman had complete faith in the words of the *rebbe*, and so he returned to the camp. But the days turned into weeks, and his situation remained the same.

Five weeks later, Mr. Friedman was waiting on line with the rest of the workers at the camp, waiting to receive his work order for the day. Finally his turn came.

"No order for you, Friedman," the officer declared. "You're summoned to the council."

"The council!" Mr. Friedman's friends were terrified. "What have you done? Why have they called you?"

A summons to the council was a one-way ticket. There was nothing more dreaded in the labor camp. It was well known: anyone who entered the council room never returned.

Knees knocking, hands shaking, Mr. Friedman hesitantly knocked on the door to the council room.

"Come in!"

The officer on duty was standing inside, looking bored. "Ah, Friedman." He rummaged through the papers on his desk, finally coming up with a pass. "Here, this is for you. You've received a discharge from the head office. You can leave the camp."

Mr. Friedman blinked. What had the officer said? Was that really a pass? Mr. Friedman took the paper with trembling fingers. Yes, it was a pass. He was free, free to leave the labor camp. And as he took his leave, Mr. Friedman whispered his gratitude to Hashem and praised the holy Bixader Rebbe, whose blessing had clearly helped him gain his freedom.

After some time, Mr. Friedman joined up with a group of Jewish Polish refugees who had witnessed firsthand the horrors of the Nazi regime. These people had arrived penniless, with nothing more than the clothes on their backs. Mr. Friedman decided to collect clothing from the Jewish storekeepers to help them return to a life of dignity. The refugees were grateful for his aid, and Mr. Friedman soon became known as a practical man who was able to get things done.

In March of 1944, the Germans entered Hungary. The Polish refugees, who were by now very friendly with Mr. Friedman, begged him to leave the country.

"We've lived through it ourselves," they insisted. "No one else will believe what we tell them, but it's the truth. You've got to get out before it's too late!"

Mr. Friedman was shaken by their words, and after careful consideration, he decided that they were right. Without losing any more time, he made his way over the border into Bucharest, Rumania.

In Rumania, Mr. Friedman met the Sassover Rebbe, the son-in-law of the Satmar Rebbe. By now, the *rebbe* knew of Mr. Friedman's reputation, and he felt that Mr. Friedman would be the right man to help at this time of crisis.

"We are expecting thousands of Jews to be fleeing here from Groszvardan and other cities in Hungary," the *rebbe* explained. "We need someone who has influence in the Rumanian government, who can convince them to let the refugees stay here.

"Dr. Ernest Martin, a Jew, is an official in the Rumanian government. If he is convinced of the importance of this cause, he can be a great help in saving many people. But you must go quickly, because he is about to leave the country."

Mr. Friedman approached Dr. Martin. "I've heard that you're planning to leave the country."

"I certainly am," Dr. Martin said tersely. "And not a moment too soon."

"I understand your desire to leave. But there are thousands of Jews who will be fleeing Hungary and will be coming to Rumania. We're afraid that the Rumanian government will force them to return to Hungary, where they will certainly be lost.

"You have the power to save thousands of lives. Won't you stay and help these people?"

Dr. Martin erupted. "Are you mad? How can I stay here any longer? My family is already out of the country. I can't lose this chance!"

"Listen to me," Mr. Friedman said calmly, unperturbed by the doctor's outburst. "You have the opportunity to save many, many people. Your family is safe. If you leave now, you will live with the knowledge that you abandoned thousands of Jews. Their deaths will be on your conscience."

But Dr. Martin remained firm. "It will mean my own life if I stay here much longer. I am not willing to throw that away."

Nothing Mr. Friedman said could make him change his mind. Finally, Mr. Friedman got up to leave. The knowledge that there was nothing more he could do to save these people brought tears to his eyes, and he quickly turned toward the door.

But Dr. Martin had seen those tears. And despite his adamant refusal, something within him was moved.

"Stop," he said suddenly.

Mr. Friedman froze with his hand on the doorknob.

Dr. Martin sat in silence. Finally he said, "Come back tomorrow. Bring me a list of all these people, and I'll see what I can do."

Mr. Friedman lost no time in putting together the list of names. The next day, he brought the list to Dr. Ernest Martin.

Dr. Martin read through the list. He recognized many of

the names—they were people from his own hometown! No longer was this a simple list of names on paper. These were real people, people who were desperately depending on him for a chance at life.

Dr. Martin reached into his pocket. "This is a ticket for the ship I'm due to travel on," he said, waving a piece of paper at Mr. Friedman.

Then Dr. Martin gripped the ticket firmly and tore it in half. He looked Mr. Friedman right in the eye. "All right, I'm staying," he said quietly. "Tell me what you want me to do."

First, Mr. Friedman asked for an office. Then he explained that he needed to arrange for ships to take all the refugees to Eretz Yisrael.

In an astonishingly short time, the ships were on their way, ready to be loaded with refugees. Arrangements were made with both the Rumanian and German governments for safe passage for these ships. Soon several ships were loaded with people and were safely on their way to Eretz Yisrael.

Even as some of the refugees left, however, more kept pouring into the country. They knew about the ships to Eretz Yisrael. And they were terrified that they would be left behind.

They began to come to Mr. Friedman, offering him money and valuables in exchange for passage on one of the ships. But Mr. Friedman was firm.

"Please, keep your money and possessions. There is room for everyone. The Rumanian government wants you to leave, so they'll make sure that no one is left behind. And once you reach Eretz Yisrael, you'll need every penny you have. So please, don't try to give me anything, and don't offer any money to any members of this committee. That's the only way to ensure the complete success of this operation."

Mr. Friedman had to repeat this speech almost every week. But he was adamant in his refusal to accept anything from the refugees. That was the only way to ensure that the work would be done solely for the sake of Heaven, which he felt was vital to the success of the mission.

There was a tremendous amount of work to be done, and Mr. Friedman needed some help. He approached two friends of his and asked if they were interested in getting involved.

"Before you answer me," he told them, "I must caution you about one thing. We are arranging ships and passage for many people to Eretz Yisrael. These people, who are desperate to get away, have already approached me with offers of gold, jewels, diamonds and money to ensure that they have a place on the ships.

"But the only way to ensure that this operation will be successful is for us to do this work completely for the sake of Heaven, without any thought of monetary compensation. Many people will be approaching you with offers of bribes. Please give me your word that you will not accept a *groshen* for your efforts."

A new transport of boats was scheduled to leave several days later. Mr. Friedman, his family, and his two new assistants had arranged to board the first ship in the transport and accompany the voyage to Eretz Yisrael. But just before the boat was due to leave, Mr. Friedman's three-year-old nephew, his sister's son, began running a high fever. The doctor declared that it would be life-threatening for the child to travel.

"In that case," Mr. Friedman said, "we are not going."

And so the ship he was to board, with two other boats traveling with it, left Rumania, leaving Mr. Friedman and his family behind.

Mr. Friedman returned to his office, determined to continue with his rescue work. A short while after he had settled down at his desk, he heard someone enter the room.

Mr. Friedman looked up and discovered a burly, heavyset man standing next to his desk.

"Can I help you?" he asked politely.

The man leaned menacingly over his desk. "I heard that those ships that just sailed had been out of commission for over forty years," he growled. "And I heard that the first ship sank.

"My son and daughter-in-law went on that ship. If it sank, let me tell you—I'll come kill you myself."

Mr. Friedman was aghast. Hundreds of people had been on that first ship! Could this be true?

He started investigating the matter. Eventually, the truth came to light. The ship had not sunk due to natural causes. The Germans had sunk the ship, thereby killing nearly everyone on board*. Although arrangements had been made with the Germans to allow the ships to get through, the Germans had discovered that illegal transactions had been performed in connection with this transport. They therefore reneged on their agreement and sank the ship.

Fortunately, the other two craft had seen what had happened to the leading ship. Since they were smaller ships which sailed closer to land, they were able to extinguish their lights and slip back to shore.

Mr. Friedman was shaken to the core. Although he was thankful to Hashem that he and his family had been saved, hundreds of Jews had perished on board that ship. Mr. Friedman could not understand it. Everything had been

---

*Interestingly, three people did survive the shipwreck, two of which were the son and daughter-in-law of the man who had originally told Mr. Friedman about the fate of the ship.

done for the sake of the *klal*, for the sake of Heaven. Why had things turned out this way?

However, Mr. Friedman's suspicions were confirmed. Indeed, there were those that submitted to their inclinations and succumbed to treachery. In an atmosphere of disloyalty and selfishness, satan lodges accusation before the heavenly court, endangering all.

From that day on, Mr. Friedman always impressed on others who were involved in *klal* work, "You must do your work *solely* for the sake of Heaven, if you truly wish to succeed."

1
ETHICAL CONDUCT

To Live as Jew
■ ■ ■

The remarkable story of a Jewish soldier's determination to remain steadfast in his faith while serving in the New York National Guard during the Vietnam era.

1
Ethical Conduct

TO LIVE AS A JEW

Mendel and Rivka Feit arrived in America in the early 1950's. Their escape from Russia led them to Boro Park, where they quickly made themselves at home. Their son Zev began going to Yeshivah Toras Emes, and he continued on to Yeshivah Kaminetz for high school.

After graduating from high school, Zev began to consider looking for a livelihood. But this was America in 1964, and the best laid plans of many young men were soon to be disrupted by the U.S. Army.

The Vietnam War had not yet begun, but the United States had sent their first observers in preparation for the battle that they knew was soon to begin. The draft was already in force.

Zev knew that full-time *yeshivah* students were exempt from the draft. But he also knew that, although he was very committed to *Yiddishkeit*, he was simply not cut out to learn on a *beis midrash* schedule. On the other hand, it would be foolhardy for Zev to allow himself to be drafted for two years. The U.S. Army was not exactly known for its *kashrus* standards, nor for its strict adherence to *Shabbos*, Torah or *mitzvos*.

The draft was affecting nearly everyone in the neighborhood in one way or another. Zev knew that he would have to take steps before his number came up. He began to think about his options.

One consideration was to join the army reserves. After all, it was only for six months, and the office was right nearby. But before jumping into anything, Zev decided to check it out.

There was a non-Jewish family that lived on Zev's block. Zev had heard that their son had signed up for the army reserves some time before, and he went to ask them about it.

"Didn't Joey sign up for six months?" he queried. "I get the impression that he's been gone for a long time."

"Yes, he has been gone a long time," Joey's father said. "In fact, he's been gone for three years."

"Three years! What happened to the six months? I thought if you sign up, you get out in six months."

"We also thought that," Joey's father admitted. "But it turns out that if you sign up for the Army Reserves, the Army has the right to take you to wherever they need you. Joey's been shipped to Berlin."

Clearly, this was not a solution. Zev had to think of some alternative.

Zev spoke to several more people. Many of them recommended the New York National Guard, which was a militia force recruited by the state. Although it was similar to the Army Reserves in that he would have to go for a six-month training course, return for five weekends, and go to a two-week retraining detail once a year for five years, it had one main advantage. While the Army Reserves soldiers could be called up individually and sent where the army needed them, National Guard soldiers could only be sent as part of their complete unit, which was unlikely to happen.

Zev was convinced. Time was growing short, so Zev and a friend decided to sign up for the National Guard the following week. That *Shabbos*, however, something happened to make Zev change his mind.

He got his draft notice.

Now there was no time to waste. It was now or never. First thing Monday morning, Zev and his friend went down to the nearest National Guard office.

"We'd like to sign up," he told the officer behind the desk.

"Fine," the man said. "Just fill out these forms here."

"Great," Zev said, scanning the forms. "How long will it take to be accepted?"

"Around three to four weeks," the man cheerfully replied.

"Three to four weeks!" Zev couldn't believe it. He would have to answer his draft notice well before then. What should he do now?

Zev thought quickly. There was another National Guard office nearby, on Bedford and Atlantic. It certainly wouldn't hurt to try them out.

Zev came striding into the office.

"I'd like to sign up," he told the officer behind the desk.

"Fine, no problem."

"Just one question. How long will it take?"

"No time at all," the officer reassured him. "We're ready when you are. You can come back for your physical on

Wednesday, and by Thursday you'll know if you passed."

It sounded good. But Zev had to check out one more thing. He took out his draft notice and showed it to the officer. "Does this cause any problems?"

"No problem at all," the man told him. "As long as you're with us, you don't have to answer your draft notice."

Zev left in a buoyant mood. All he and his friend had to do was pass the physical on Wednesday, and then they'd be in.

Wednesday evening, Zev and his friend came for their physical. Zev went through one door, while his friend went through the other door. After a short while, Zev was finished, and he went back out to wait for his friend. But the minutes went by without any sign of him. People who had arrived after they had come in were already finished, but his friend had simply disappeared.

Zev finally decided to check it out. He went back through the door and looked around for someone in charge.

"Excuse me," he said to a man in an official-looking white coat. "I'm looking for someone." Zev mentioned his friend's name, and the man brusquely pointed to a cot in the corner.

Zev apprehensively went over. His friend was lying down on the cot, his face pale.

"What happened?" Zev asked in concern.

One of the doctors standing nearby heard his question. "Your friend there has high blood pressure," he told Zev. "I guess all the testing got him nervous, which made his blood pressure go even higher, until he fainted."

The doctor looked at Zev thoughtfully. "I may as well tell you now. He isn't going to pass."

Zev's heart fell. He had been hoping to have some company in the National Guard. But now it seemed that he would have to be on his own.

The next day, the news came. Zev had passed his physical. But his friend, as the doctor had predicted, had not. Zev would be going alone.

It was in early August that Zev—now called Willy—received his orders. He packed his bags, got on the bus and went off to Fort Dix, New Jersey—all the while keeping his *yarmulke* firmly on his head. Zev had always been known as the "Yerushalmi" where he lived, since he was one of the few people in his neighborhood who insisted on wearing his *yarmulke* at all times. Despite the fact that he was going into the army, he had no intention of changing his behavior.

The bus finally arrived at Fort Dix. A sergeant jumped on the bus as soon as it stopped, and began shouting, "You have one minute to get off this bus, and you've already used up thirty seconds!"

The rush began. Everyone grabbed his duffle bag and tried to get off the bus. Two sergeants were standing next to the exit, watching the disorderly exodus. Willy got jammed in the shuffle, and as he got off the bus, he lost his balance and his duffle bag started to fall. He quickly flipped it back over his shoulder—not noticing the sergeant standing next to him, right in the way of the duffle bag.

It was a perfect hit. The sergeant fell to the floor without realizing what had hit him. The crowd was so packed that no one noticed what had happened. Willy prudently continued to walk away from the bus.

The sergeant finally struggled to his feet. His uniform was torn and tattered, and there was a bruise beginning to form on his face. "Just wait until I find out who did this to me!" he yelled.

Fortunately for Willy, the sergeant never did find out.

The new recruits were brought into a reception building,

where they were given uniforms and assigned to their platoons. An officer with a thick Southern accent called out each name, and the named recruit responded.

The officer called out one name, but no one answered.

"Why don't you spell out the name?" Willy suggested.

"Good idea," the officer agreed. "F-E-I-T," he called at the top of his lungs.

"Oh, that's me," Willy told him.

"Why didn't you answer me before?"

"I didn't recognize what you were saying before."

"Oh, okay." The officer scratched his head. "Anyway, you have a meeting with the chaplain."

Willy went off to find the chaplain, who explained to him the rights he had as a Jew in the army. Willy then returned to the main hall, where he was issued his uniform and assigned to his platoon. Unfortunately, the platoon's commanding officers looked familiar—they were the two sergeants who had greeted him at the bus.

The first Friday afternoon at Fort Dix, Willy asked for permission to go back to his barracks to prepare for *Shabbos*, which was his right according to army law.

"No way!" the sergeant told him. "You can't leave here for any reason."

"I'm sorry, sir," Willy said firmly. "I'll have to see the commanding officer, then. I'll tell him that I have to leave for Sabbath observance."

The sergeant grew visibly upset. "No one sees the captain!" he retorted.

"I'm sorry, but that's not what the chaplain told me."

Willy knew that he was on dangerous ground. Using the chain of command was the one sure way of getting results in the army—but it was also never supposed to be used. Still, at this point, he had no choice.

The sergeant was taken aback. "Oh, really," he snapped. "Who's this chaplain you keep on talking about?"

"Well," Willy said, feigning ignorance, "he wears a gold oak leaf on his shirt*, and anyone who disobeys his orders gets demoted to a private."

The sergeant paled. "Never mind that," he said hastily. "I'll go to the captain now and check if he'll see you."

After a short wait, Willy was called into the captain's office.

"What seems to be the problem?" the officer asked.

"I'm a Sabbath observer," Willy explained. "I have to be excused now so I can attend Friday night services. I will also need to be excused for the whole day tomorrow."

The captain frowned. "I wasn't told about this."

"The chaplain told me to speak to my commanding officer. I spoke to the chaplain before I was assigned to my platoon, so he had no way of knowing whom to contact. I'll be able to tell the chaplain tonight, so by Monday you'll have confirmation."

"That sounds all right to me," the captain agreed. "You are excused until tomorrow night."

Willy's barracks was situated at the edge of the camp, three miles away from the main parade grounds, where the *shul* was located. Willy got ready for *Shabbos* and ordered a cab to take him to *shul*. Along the way, he took careful note of the route—since he would have to walk back that night.

Davening and eating the Friday night meal took some time, and it was quite late before Willy set out on the return trip. The camp was dark, and the night hid most of the landmarks that Willy had memorized. But he really had no choice. And so he set out with a prayer on his lips for Divine

---

A gold oak leaf signifies a major.

guidance back to his barracks.

It was eleven-thirty in the evening before Willy finally reached his barracks. Lights-out was officially at ten o'clock, and the bed check had already been taken. Willy walked up quietly, but the two sergeants in charge came running out.

"Who's there?" they called.

"Who are you?" Willy retorted.

"Oh, it's Feit!" one of the sergeants exclaimed. "You're in trouble, Feit. You've been AWOL (absent without leave)."

"I'm really sorry, but I couldn't get back any earlier. I had to walk back because it's my Sabbath."

"Where were you walking from?" the sergeant asked suspiciously.

"From the chapel," Willy replied.

"The chapel? Where's that?"

"It's near the main parade grounds," Willy offered.

That didn't strike a bell, either. "Where's that located?" they wanted to know.

Willy thought hard. He finally recalled that there was a beer hall near the parade grounds. "It's near the main beer hall," he told them.

"You're kidding!" the sergeant said in amazement. "You walked all the way from the beer hall?"

"Yes, I did," Willy told them. "I'm not allowed to drive on my Sabbath."

The sergeant shook his head in amazement. "If you were willing to walk all that way for your Sabbath, I'm certainly not going to stop you from entering the barracks."

And after that, the two sergeants never gave Willy any trouble about his absences on Friday night.

■ ■ ■

Willy soon learned that there are three ways to get things

done: the right way, the wrong way and the army way.

The Jewish chaplain was given an assistant who turned out to be non-Jewish, while the Catholic chaplain's assistant was a Jew. After several weeks, the non-Jewish assistant came over to Willy.

"I don't understand what I'm doing here," he complained. "I have to prepare the ark, put the books away and take care of the synagogue. I'm not even a Jew! Why should the Catholic chaplain get a Jew to work for him, while I'm stuck over here?"

Willy went over to the chaplain. "Why is there a Jew working for the Catholic chaplain, and a non-Jew working for you?" he asked.

The chaplain shrugged. "That's the army way."

"That's because the people in the army who arranged this don't know any better," Willy argued. "But you do know better. Why don't you go talk to the Catholic chaplain? I'm sure he'll agree to switch."

The chaplain had to agree with Willy's reasoning. The Catholic chaplain also agreed, and so the two of them made the switch.

Before long, though, Willy realized that the Jewish chaplain might have been better off with the non-Jewish assistant. The non-Jew had been religious, at least, but the Jewish assistant was completely non-observant. Still, there was the hope that he might take the chance to learn what it means to be a Jew.

The first *Shabbos* the new *shammos* was on the job, the chaplain did not come to *shul*, since he lived far away. Still, the *shul* was full that *Shabbos*, as all the Jewish soldiers exercised their rights to have the day off.

After *Shacharis*, the *shammos* approached Willy. "You're a *yeshivah* boy. Can you give the sermon this week? The chaplain didn't show up today, and we have a full crowd."

Willy was taken aback. "I'm not a rabbi. Not only that, I don't even know what this week's *sidrah* is! I've spent the whole week running up and down mountains, and you tend to lose track of things that way. There's no way I can do it."

Willy thought that he had taken care of that idea. But a few minutes later, the *shammos* went up to the pulpit. "Private Feit has agreed to deliver the sermon today," he announced.

Now Willy was in for it. In the few seconds it would take for him to reach the pulpit, he had to open his *Chumash*, recall the *parshah* and put together a speech.

Well, Willy got up there, took a deep breath, and began to speak. He listened in amazement to the words that flowed from his mouth. He glanced around the *shul* as he spoke, and he noticed that people seemed to be enjoying the sermon.

This was quite different from the usual reaction to the chaplain's sermon. When the chaplain faced the left side of the *shul*, the people on the right walked out; and when he faced the right side of the *shul*, the people on the left walked out.

After his speech was over, many of the congregants came over to him. "That was excellent," they congratulated him. "We really enjoyed it."

From then on, Willy was the first choice to give the sermon on *Shabbos*.

One week, Willy was giving the sermon when he noticed the chaplain in the *shul*. Afterwards, Willy went over to him. "Why didn't you give the sermon yourself?" he asked.

"I've heard such wonderful things about your sermons," the chaplain told him. "I wanted to hear one for myself. Tell me, what do you say that's different from my sermons? How do you get everyone to listen to you?"

"It's simple," Willy told him. "When you speak, you speak to me—as a *yeshivah bachur*. But when I speak, I speak to the others on *their* level—so it's something they can relate to."

■ ■ ■

Willy had the job of giving out the *aliyos* to the Torah. One *Shabbos*, he approached a man and asked him for his name to be called up to the Torah.

"Oh, I'm sorry, but I'm not Jewish," the man told him.

"If you're not Jewish, what are you doing here?" Willy asked in bewilderment.

"I'm a seventh-day adventist," the man explained, "and this is the only chapel that's open on Saturdays."

From then on, whenever Willy approached a new person to offer him an *aliyah*, he always began with the question, "Are you Jewish?"

■ ■ ■

Many different people passed through the chapel. Among them was a non-religious family who lived near the base. Although they were not observant, they wanted to show their children something of their Jewish heritage.

One of the boys was approaching *bar-mitzvah*, and the chaplain was giving him lessons. Harold was a brilliant boy, and he became very close to Willy. He would sit there while Willy and the chaplain learned *Chumash* together, and he stayed for the *zemiros* when they ate.

One day, Harold came over to Willy with a serious request. "I want to start learning Torah," he told him.

"Well, then, you'll have to go to a *yeshivah*," Willy said.

The chaplain, who was also very impressed with Harold, made arrangements for the boy to enter *yeshivah*.

After six months, Willy was finished with his basic training, but he still had to return to Fort Dix for five weekends. It was during that first weekend back that he saw Harold again.

Harold had become a real *ben Torah*. In fact, he was concerned about staying in his parents' home for *Pesach*. "Can I come to your house?" he begged Willy.

Willy didn't feel that it would be right. He convinced Harold that he would be better off staying by his parents for *Yom Tov*. Harold eventually agreed, but on condition that he would be in charge of the *kashrus*. He bought new pots and pans and converted the entire kitchen.

During another weekend on base, Harold's mother came over to Willy. "Look what you've done to my family," she said bitterly. "First my pots and pans weren't good enough, and now the *yeshivah* is complaining about him. I got this letter written in Hebrew from the school dean. I can't even read it, but I'm sure there's something wrong."

Willy glanced at the letter for a minute. Then he smiled.

"This is great news," he told her. "Let me translate it for you."

The letter said that Harold had won a set of *Gemaras* for learning twelve *blatt Gemara* by heart. And this was a boy who hadn't even known the *aleph-beis* a year before!

Harold grew up to be a big *talmid chacham*, and he brought his whole family with him to *Yiddishkeit*.

■ ■ ■

Fort Dix was situated next to McGuire Air Force Base. There was a disbursement camp in the base, where people who were in transit stayed until they were given their new orders.

The Jews who came to the disbursement camp generally

became a part of the *shul* family. One person who showed up did not even know that he was Jewish. He explained that his mother had been Jewish, but she had converted to Catholicism during World War II to save her life.

This man had come from Texas. He was supposed to be transferred elsewhere, but when he showed the officer in charge his documents, they told him to wait until his shipping documents came in. Since he had nothing better to do, he came to *shul* and listened to the chaplain's sermon.

Some time went by, but the man's shipping orders never arrived. While this meant that he was safe for the time being, he also was not receiving his pay. After a while, he completely ran out of money. He wasn't even able to clean his khaki summer uniform, and so he walked around the base wearing his dark-green winter uniform.

This went on for six months. With little to do, the soldier began taking some classes in *Yiddishkeit*, and he slowly began to become *frum*. The chaplain also gave him some small jobs to do to keep him busy.

One day, the chaplain asked him to clean the brass fire extinguisher. The soldier went outside and began polishing it. As he worked, he noticed a jeep approaching. The car began passing in front of him, and he realized with a start that there was a general in the car.

The army rule is that if a commanding officer passes by, you must stand at attention and salute. However, if something is in your hands, you do not need to salute.

The soldier had forgotten that rule, though, so he tried to salute with the fire extinguisher in his hands. As he passed the extinguisher from one hand to another, he accidentally turned it upside down, which somehow activated the foam.

Unfortunately, the fire extinguisher was pointing right at the general.

Foam shot out of the fire extinguisher, coating the general from top to bottom. The officer stopped the jeep and slowly got out of the car. He stalked up to the soldier, who was still standing at attention, and looked him up and down.

"Soldier," he snapped, "you're wearing the wrong uniform."

"I don't have any money to clean my summer uniform," the man meekly replied.

"You're supposed to make your paycheck stretch," the general said.

"Well, I would," the soldier said, "but I haven't been getting a paycheck."

"What do you mean? Why haven't you been paid?"

"I don't know," the soldier admitted. "But I've been here for six months, and I haven't received even one single paycheck."

The general looked at him for a moment. "Soldier," he said quietly, "if you're telling the truth, then tomorrow you'll get your money. But if you're lying—then tomorrow, you'll be in jail."

After a little investigation, the general discovered that the soldier had been telling the truth. Somehow, he had been ignored the entire time that he had been on base. The general arranged for the soldier to receive his back pay, which added up to several thousand dollars.

Unfortunately, the general also discovered the shipping orders that had been mislaid—a transfer to Korea.

The soldier took an emotional leave of his friends in the *shul*. He made arrangements at McGuire Air Force Base to "rent a parachute," which meant taking an uncomfortable, no-frills flight to his destination. This allowed him to save most of his travel allowance. He then went to New York and bought *sefarim* with all of his money, which he took along to Korea with him.

After some time in Korea, the soldier discovered that there was no chaplain in Saigon, and he volunteered his services. Eventually, the men at the Fort Dix *shul* lost track of him. One day, however, the chaplain received a letter from overseas.

The soldier had unfortunately been killed. Apparently, he had put down his friends at the *shul* as his next of kin— so close had been the spiritual bond that had developed between them. While he did not live long after his return to *Yiddishkeit*, he died at peace with himself, secure with the knowledge that he had returned to Hashem and His Torah.

■ ■ ■

Willy was once driving in an army truck with an Italian. As they drove, the truck hit a bump, and the madonna that the Italian was wearing turned over. Willy noticed that there was a *magen david* on the back of it.

"Did you see that?" the Italian asked him.

"Yes, I did. Is that a good luck charm or something?"

"No," the man told him. "I'm wearing it because I'm going to be a Jew."

"You're going to be a Jew? Why do you want to do that?"

"I'm wearing this madonna in respect for my mother," the man explained. "But as soon as I'm out of the army, the madonna goes, and the G-d of Israel is mine. I learned from a rabbi in Brooklyn that I have to have respect for my parents. So as long as I'm near my mother, I'll wear this. But when I get out of the army, I'll be moving to California, and then I'm converting."

"But why do you want to do that?" Willy asked again.

"I was brought up as a religious Catholic," the Italian

said, "but every time I asked the priest a question about something that didn't make sense to me, he would brush it off. 'You're not allowed to question, you must have faith,' he would say.

"Well, I had a few Jewish friends, and they didn't mind answering my questions. I started talking to an Orthodox rabbi, and he didn't mind either. After hearing a few answers, I realized that I'm practicing a religion that was adapted from another religion. Here we are, waiting for G-d to get angry at the Jews and adopt us. Why not just join the Jewish people and be done with it? There's no reason to be a second-class citizen if I can go first class."

■ ■ ■

One day, a non-religious Jew came over to Willy.

"Do you mind if I ask you some questions?" he said. "You might find them insulting."

"Well, it depends," Willy told him. "Are they insulting to me, or insulting to my religion?"

"Let me explain," the man said. "You see, I'm getting married to a Catholic girl. She's religious, but I come from a completely non-observant family. She thinks we should study both religions carefully to decide which one is right. She doesn't want to have G-dless children.

"Well, after looking into it, she's decided that Judaism is the right religion. Now she's telling me that she has to light candles every Friday night, that she has to cover her hair, that I'm not allowed to work or smoke on Saturdays. I never heard of these laws. Is this true?"

Willy smiled. "Yes," he told him. "They are all true."

Every week, the man would come to Willy with more questions, which he was more than happy to answer. As the man's fiance became closer to Judaism, her family, who were devout Catholics, became more and more concerned. Eventually, they insisted that she give up her search—or they would have nothing more to do with her. The man's family, who were completely assimilated Jews, also insisted that their son give up his quest for *Yiddishkeit*—or they would have nothing more to do with him. Eventually, the pressure from both sides became unbearable, and so the two of them decided to leave the army and move to California, where they would have the peace of mind to concentrate on the major decisions they were considering.

The man's fiance first converted through a Reform rabbi. She wasn't satisfied, though, so she approached a Conservative rabbi. But that didn't work either. She soon realized that she needed to talk to an Orthodox rabbi.

The rabbi tried to dissuade her from her decision. But she was adamant, and eventually, he arranged her conversion. The man was so impressed with his future wife's determination that he, too, accepted upon himself to keep the laws of the Torah.

■ ■ ■

Sometimes, Willy was lucky enough to work in the mess hall, where he was able to get as many vegetables as he wanted. In general, though, keeping kosher was not very easy in the army. Still, there was one incident that made Willy very grateful for this *mitzvah*.

At one point, Willy's job was to empty out the pots after the midday meal so they could be washed. The other soldiers had already returned to their field assignments, and Willy was busy emptying out a huge soup pot. Suddenly he noticed something strange on the bottom of the pot. He reached in and pulled out an empty can of detergent.

Willy immediately ran over to the mess sergeant. "Look

what I found!" he yelled, brandishing the can.

"So, what's the big deal?" the sergeant asked impatiently.

"It was on the bottom of the soup pot," Willy informed him.

The sergeant stared at him. "You're kidding, right?"

"No, I'm serious. That's where it was."

The sergeant's face changed colors. "We've been poisoned!" he yelled. "Get that stuff out of your system!" And he charged straight for the washroom. The rest of the kitchen staff quickly followed suit, until Willy was the only one left standing there.

Just then, the captain walked in. "Hey, where is everyone?" he asked with a frown.

"Well, uh, they're all in the washroom, sir."

"What are they doing there?"

"You see, I found an empty can of detergent on the bottom of the soup pot," Willy explained. "After I told the sergeant about it, they all ran straight in there—and they still haven't come out."

"Please call the mess sergeant out," the captain requested.

Willy went to the washroom to get the sergeant, who was looking somewhat the worse for wear. The sergeant came over to where the captain was waiting.

"Is this soldier telling the truth?" the captain asked him.

"Sir, I've been in there since he told me about it—believe me, he's telling the truth!"

The captain immediately went over to a phone and ordered all the soldiers in the field to return to their barracks. "Those soldiers may need immediate medical attention!" he barked into the receiver.

Indeed, the soldiers were very ill for a long time. That is, all except for Willy—who alone had kept the *mitzvah* of eating kosher.

■ ■ ■

Willy was *davening* in *shul* one *Shabbos* morning when he started feeling feverish. As the day wore on, he felt worse and worse, and when *Shabbos* was over he could barely walk. He managed to get out of the *shul* to call a cab to take him back to the barracks.

When he managed to stagger into the barracks, the sergeant greeted him at the door. "You're the last one left, Feit. Here's your pass. Everyone else has already left for their day off."

"Forget the pass," Willy groaned. "I want to see a doctor."

"Oh, come on," the sergeant scoffed. "You can go to the doctor on Monday. Why would you want to waste your day off visiting the doctor?"

But Willy was adamant, so the sergeant called two guards to take him to the hospital, since the clinic was already closed.

At the hospital, the guards waited while a nurse took Willy's temperature. She studied the thermometer with a frown, then glanced up at the guards.

"Why are you still here?" she asked.

"The sergeant told us to take Willy to the bus when he leaves," they told her.

"Well," she said bluntly, "you'll be waiting for about a week. He's got a fever of 104 degrees!"

Willy was admitted to the hospital and given plenty of liquids to avoid dehydration. The fever had broken by the following morning, but Willy was still in no shape to go anywhere. It was clear that he would be staying in the hospital for at least a few more days.

With his fever gone, Willy began to grow hungry. But he didn't have his food supplies with him, and there was no kosher food available in the hospital. It was Sunday, the soldiers' day off, and there was no one for him to get in touch with. Willy was stuck.

Willy was growing more and more ravenous. He thought he was hallucinating when he heard a voice call, "Where is Feit?" He raised his head and looked around. "Over here," he motioned.

A nurse came running over. "Here, this is for you." She gave him an ice pack and cold compresses.

Willy stared at them in disbelief. "What's all this for? I'm not the one with the fever! Give it to the guy next to me. He's really burning up."

"Sorry," the nurse refused. "They said to give it to Feit, and that's you."

With that, she turned and left.

"Great," Willy muttered. "Here I need food, and they try to give me pneumonia."

He took the ice pack and threw it under his bed. Then he lay there, trying to ignore his empty stomach.

A few hours later, the nurse came running in. "Are you okay?" she gasped. "Those ice packs weren't for you, they were for the other guy! You might get pneumonia!"

"Don't worry, I didn't keep them," Willy told her. "They're under my bed."

The nurse smiled in relief and left the room.

A moment later, he again heard someone calling, "Where is Feit?"

"Should I answer?" Willy wondered. "Who knows what they'll try to do to me this time!"

Again, the voice called, "Where is Feit?"

"Over here," Willy finally called.

A woman came over and presented him with a tray of food. Willy looked at it with astonishment. It was a sealed kosher meal! Where had it come from? How had the hospital known that he was Jewish?

Willy felt an extra sense of gratitude to Hashem as he made a *berachah* and ate his long-awaited meal. But it wasn't until the next day that he discovered who had engineered the whole thing.

One of the members of the *shul*, a *frum* dentist, came to visit him on Monday morning.

"How are you doing, Willy?" he asked with a smile. "Did you get the meal I sent you?"

"You sent me that meal?" Willy asked in astonishment. "How did you know I was here?"

"Some time ago, I took it upon myself to check the patient list at the hospital every day. If there are any Jewish names on it, I order them a kosher meal. So when I saw your name yesterday, I made sure that you got your meal!"

Once again, Hashem had helped Willy keep kosher — even in a most difficult situation.

■ ■ ■

One Friday night, Willy was on his way back to the barracks after the *Shabbos* meal was over. As he passed the main stockade, which contained a military prison, military police suddenly jumped out of the bushes and surrounded him. Apparently, there had been a prison break earlier, and the guards were hunting for the culprits. When they saw Willy pass by, they thought they had their man.

Several rifles were suddenly pointed in Willy's direction.

"Identify yourself!" one of the soldiers barked.

Willy, of course, was not carrying his I.D. card on *Shabbos*. "I don't have my I.D. on me," he tried to explain.

"It's him," one of the guards muttered. "Let's go get him!"

"Just one minute." One of the officers came closer to Willy. "Can you give us any reason to believe that you're not an escaped prisoner?"

Willy thought fast. He remembered once seeing the prisoners marching by in old work clothing. "Look at my uniform," he said. "I've never been in prison, but I doubt this is the way prisoners dress in jail."

"Hmm." The officer continued to look dubious.

"Look," Willy said desperately. "The only reason I don't have my I.D. is that I'm a religious Jew, and I'm not allowed to carry on my Sabbath."

The officer nodded. "Yes, I'm aware that religious Jews do those things. And you're right about the uniform. Okay, I guess you're in the clear."

Willy breathed a silent blessing to Hashem as the soldiers melted away into the darkness, allowing him to continue on his journey.

■ ■ ■

In the army, wearing a hat is only permitted outdoors. When a soldier enters a building, he is required to remove his head covering. This applies to a *yarmulke* as well. But Willy still insisted on wearing his *yarmulke* at all times.

Once, Willy entered the mess hall and, as usual, removed his hat and put on his *yarmulke*. He sat down at a table with the Brooklyn boys, who already knew him and always gave him their vegetables, since he ate very little else.

Suddenly the head sergeant, Elis B. Daily, walked in. He immediately spotted Willy's *yarmulke*. Instead of confronting Willy right away, the sergeant started circling his table. With each circle, Willy could feel himself growing more and more tense. The other men at the table were also frozen with fear.

Finally the sergeant stopped. His finger shot out and pointed at the *yarmulke*. "You know," he shouted, "I got one of them."

"What?" Willy said incredulously.

"Yeah, I got one of those hats in my drawer."

Then the sergeant pulled out his dog tags. On his chain there was a *magen david*, a cross and a buddha.

"You see," he said, pointing, "I got a star of David."

"Yes, I see," Willy said weakly. "In fact, I see you've got them all."

"That's right," the sergeant confirmed. "I don't know who G-d is, but I want to be on His side. So I'm taking no chances. I'm on everyone's side!"

From that day on, the sergeant was always on Willy's side whenever he had a run-in with the other officers.

■ ■ ■

The soldiers' barracks were set up according to their last names. Feit found himself sleeping next to Farrow, a nice Jewish fellow who liked Willy and became closer to *Yiddishkeit* through their relationship. Willy wasn't so lucky with his other bunkmate, though. The fellow who slept in the upper bunk was Fernandez, a real anti-Semite who would do anything to get at Willy.

Shortly before *Rosh Hashanah*, Willy was due to get a pass together with the other Jewish soldiers to go home for *yom tov*. Fernandez knew about the upcoming holiday, and he had an idea.

He went over to two of the sergeants who also had it in

for Willy. "We can make some good money on these Jews," he told them. "They have to get to New York by a certain time. If you hold onto the passes until it's too late to get transportation to the bus, they'll have to find another way to get there. I have a car, so they'll need to use my services. I'll charge them a lot of money, and we'll split it."

The sergeants liked the idea, and they shook on the deal.

Somehow, word got out, and Willy heard about what the sergeants were planning. He went over to one of them.

"If I don't get to the bus on time, I just won't go home at all."

"Don't worry," the sergeant told him. "Fernandez has a car. He can take you."

"Twelve people need to get on that bus," Willy told him. "Fernandez can only fit three in his car. There's no way we'll all make it. So I just won't go home."

"But you have to go home," the sergeant said nervously.

"That's right. But I can't go home, can I? And you'll have to explain to the officer in charge, Sergeant Daily, why I didn't make the bus. If he asks me why I didn't go home, I'll tell him it's because you held back the passes."

The sergeant made sure to give out the passes extra early so there would be no complaints, and Willy made it home in plenty of time for *yom tov*.

■ ■ ■

One week, the sergeant decided to make room inspection in middle of the week, instead of on Saturday, which was the usual procedure. Willy discovered that he had a problem. Somehow, all his hand towels had been disappearing, and now he didn't have a towel for inspection. With no recourse, Willy asked Fernandez to lend him one of his hand towels, and Fernandez kindly agreed.

After the inspection, Fernandez asked Willy for his towel back.

"I don't have your towel," Willy told him.

"What do you mean?" Fernandez yelled. "I gave you one of my towels for the inspection!"

"Actually, you didn't give me your towel," Willy told him.

"What do you mean?" Fernandez exclaimed. He turned to the other soldiers in the bunk. "This guy says I didn't give him a towel. Did any of you see me give him a towel?"

"Yeah," one of the soldiers said. "I saw you give him a towel."

"Several other men in the bunk voiced their agreement.

"You see?" Fernandez turned to Willy triumphantly.

"I didn't say that you didn't give me a towel," Willy told him.

"I said that you didn't give me your towel." Willy turned to the other soldiers in the bunk. "Look at the towel this guy lent me. For some reason, it has my I.D. numbers on it."

A hush fell over the bunk as all the men turned to stare at Fernandez.

"I'm not the only one who's been missing towels," Willy went on. "I think we now know who the theif is."

Fernandez turned red with embarrassment, and never started up with Willy again.

■ ■ ■

Willy's two sergeants always took bribes. They were even known to threaten soldiers with jail sentences if they didn't get the money that they demanded.

One day, a friend of Willy's came over to him in a very agitated mood. "Listen to what happened!" he blurted out.

Earlier that day, this soldier was coming off the rifle

range. The rule was that no one was allowed to leave the rifle range with any leftover ammunition. As the soldier passed the sergeant on his way out, the sergeant made him stand at attention. Then the sergeant put his hands in the soldier's pockets—and took out bullets!

"He told me to give him money," Willy's friend concluded, "or else he would report me and send me to jail."

"Did you really take out those bullets?" Willy asked.

"No, the sergeant framed me. He had the bullets in his palm and pretended that he took them out of my pocket."

"Then you should fight it," Willy told him. "Don't give in to him."

But Willy's friend was frightened, and he ended up giving the sergeant the money.

One day, Willy was coming off the rifle range when the same sergeant made him stand at attention. Willy knew what was coming next.

"I'm going through your pockets," the sergeant told him.

"No, you're not," Willy told him.

The sergeant jerked his hands back. "What are you talking about?"

"If you want to see what's in my pockets, I'll empty them for you," Willy said. "But don't you put your hands in my pockets."

"Oh, yeah?" the sergeant said, regaining his composure. "And what are you going to do about it?"

"Look," said Willy. "There are a lot of witnesses here. If you pull bullets out of my pockets, I will say that you planted them there, and I'll take you to a court martial."

"Oh, really," the sergeant sneered. "And who do you think they'll believe? They'll listen to a sergeant before they listen to any ordinary soldier!"

"Ordinarily, you'd be right," Willy admitted. "The difference is that this time, I'll have all the other soldiers on my side. They'll testify that you did it to them, too. And you won't have it easy if they find you guilty. The army doesn't like people like you."

The sergeant backed down. He muttered something under his breath as he turned and left.

Back at the bunk, Willy's friend asked him what had happened. When Willy told him the story, his friend quickly spread the news to the rest of the soldiers. And that was the sergeant's last attempt at bribery in that platoon.

■ ■ ■

After eight weeks, Willy was switched to a more advanced platoon. While many of the men were sent away to different states, Willy was fortunate enough to advance to a unit at Fort Dix.

Willy always tried to avoid doing any unnecessary work, often by taking on an easy task to avoid a more difficult one. For example, the soldiers once had to go to a distant site, and someone was needed to load up the truck. Willy immediately volunteered. While he knew that the loading would take half an hour of work, he also knew that he would be able to ride on the truck to the site, while the other men would have to run there.

After a while, the sergeant of the platoon realized that Willy was always ahead of the game. One day, he came over to Willy.

"You know, Feit," he said seriously, "you've been managing to get away with as little work as possible. But by doing that, you're missing out on a lot of valuable skills that you're going to need.

"In a few days, we'll be going out on a 'twenty-seven

hour problem.' We'll be out in the woods in the wintertime, and it's freezing out there. Everything you've learned during the past fifteen weeks in the army will be needed for your survival. People like you, who didn't bother learning and doing things the right way, will get hurt."

"I'm not worried about that," Willy told him.

The sergeant raised his eyebrows. "You're not worried about getting hurt?"

"You see," Willy explained, "you have to worry about yourself and all the other soldiers in the platoon. But I'm only concerned about what G-d wants from me. If G-d wants me to get hurt, I'll get hurt; and if He doesn't want me to get hurt, I'll be fine. He is the one in charge of me."

"Oh, really," the sergeant said angrily. "I guess we'll wait and see!"

Several days later, the sergeant came over to Willy with an angry expression on his face. "Just how did you accomplish this?" he asked in annoyance.

"What are you talking about?" Willy retorted.

"I got a notice from the chaplain that all Jewish personnel are invited to a Chanukah party tonight. You know, there are a lot of Jewish soldiers I could hold back, but the chaplain would certainly notice if you weren't there. So I really don't have a choice. You're officially excused from tonight's twenty-seven hour problem."

Willy smiled. "You see? You take care of yourself, and G-d will take care of me."

That evening, the thermometer went below zero. Willy took a cab back from the party, and he nearly froze in the short time it took him to reach the car.

"Why don't you take me behind the barracks?" he suggested to the cab driver. "It's a shorter walk from there to my bunk."

The driver did as he was told, and in a few minutes, Willy was back in his barracks. All the other soldiers were out in the woods, and Willy enjoyed the warmth of the barracks as he settled down to sleep.

At five o'clock in the morning, one of the other Jewish soldiers in the barracks shook him awake. "What are you doing here, Willy?" his friend asked incredulously. "You're supposed to be working!"

The soldier went on to explain that when all the other Jewish personnel returned to the barracks after the party, they were met by an officer at the front door. "Since the other guys were all out in the cold, they felt it wasn't fair for us to go to sleep in the barracks. So they gave us all jobs to do. How did you manage to luck out?"

Willy told his friend how he had come in the back instead of through the front door. "No problem, though," he reassured him. "I'll be glad to do my job now!"

And after a good night's sleep, Willy found it easy to smile as he worked, until the rest of the men came back from the field.

■ ■ ■

One sergeant named Valentine was a real soldier's soldier. He had volunteered to join the army and had gone to Vietnam before anyone else even knew where Vietnam was.

One day, he came over to Willy. "You know, Jews are the worst soldiers in the world."

"Is that so?" Willy said to him. "Who told you that?"

"I say so," Valentine told him.

"Well, I've got news for you," Willy said. "According to the Pentagon, the Israeli army is the most powerful army in the world relative to its size. And all the soldiers in it are Jews."

Well, that made Valentine back off a little. Valentine was a real army man, and the Pentagon was his Bible.

Valentine then tried a different tack. "Well, the American Jew is the worst soldier in the world."

"Just one minute here. The Pentagon says that the most Medal of Honor winners are Mexican Americans. Did you know that?"

Valentine shook his head. So Willy took the plunge.

"And they also say that the second place winners are Jews!"

"Really?" Valentine said. "I didn't know that. Well, what I meant is that you are the worst soldier in the world."

"Oh, sure," Willy said. "I won't disagree with that. I didn't come here to become a warrior; I just don't want to go to Vietnam. But if you mean me, then why are you attacking my whole religion?"

Valentine realized that he wouldn't get anywhere with Willy and walked away, defeated.

■ ■ ■

The army schedule was very intense. From early morning until late at night, the soldiers had to be out training in the field. This gave Willy a problem about *davening*. With no other choice, Willy would get up shortly before the other soldiers did and immediately put on his *tefillin*. Then he would *daven* a little bit before he had to get ready to go out in the field. He would always bring along a *siddur* and *Chumash*, and he would finish *davening* during his ten-minute breaks.

During his first eight weeks at Fort Dix, Willy was among other New Yorkers. So while his *tefillin* did elicit some comments, the other soldiers had seen them before, and weren't too shocked by them. But after the first two months of training were up, Willy was transferred to a more advanced platoon in another area of Fort Dix. And he had no way of knowing who his bunkmates would be.

Willy arrived at his new barracks on a Friday afternoon. It was getting late, and there was no time to get unpacked before *Shabbos*. So he left his luggage on one side and went off to *shul*.

When he got back to the barracks late that night, Willy was told that all the beds had already been taken. "Somehow, we're short one bed, and you got left out," the sergeant in charge told him. "You'll have to take a separate room on the side here until we get you a bed."

Naturally, Willy was thrilled. He would be able to put on his *tefillin* in private, with no one the wiser. But this happy situation only lasted for four weeks. Eventually, the sergeant got another bed in the barracks, and Willy had to bunk with the others.

Willy's new platoon was made up of soldiers who had strong ties to the Ku Klux Klan. He himself shared a cubicle with three other soldiers, two of whom were associated with the KKK. Naturally, Willy was terrified to even take out his *tefillin* when they were around. He would always cautiously don his *tefillin* when those two were asleep.

One morning, as Willy was wearing his *tefillin*, the two Klan members woke up extra early. They took one look at Willy in his *tefillin* and started yelling loud enough to wake up all the men in the barracks.

"Hey, look, these Jews can put on and take off their horns! They're removable!"

Willy was very embarrassed. But he remained unfazed.

Now that the truth was out, Willy was afraid that he would be in for it. But his bunkmates discovered that it would be to their advantage to befriend Willy, instead of poking fun at him. These two, it turned out, enjoyed drinking even more than they enjoyed making fun of Jews. Since inspection was always held on a Saturday, Willy was never around, and that meant that his locker was never inspected. Willy's roommates asked if they could store their whiskey in his locker during inspection, and he agreed.

This was the start of a better relationship. From then on, Willy was able to put on his *tefillin* without the fear of being bothered by anyone.

■ ■ ■

After his six months were up, Willy was allowed to return home, but he was required to spend two weeks a year on a tour of duty in Watertown, N.Y., about twenty-five miles from the Canadian border. During one session, the soldiers were told to dig foxholes. Since they were two-man foxholes, Willy and another fellow named Rosenberg were set up as a team.

It was a hot, sunny day, but Willy and his friend were positioned under a tree, and they were enjoying the cool shade as they worked. But the sergeant in charge wasn't fond of Willy, and he decided to assign him some extra work.

"Hey, Feit," he called. "I have an assignment for you."

Willy's new job would be to go into the field and set up land mines and booby traps for the enemy. Planes would fly over the field and drop sacks of flour on the soldiers, and the men would need to dodge the "bombs" while avoiding the land mines.

The job was very tedious, and Willy had a hard time staying alert as he worked under the hot sun. After several hours of slaving away in the heat, Willy was furious.

When the job was finally done, Willy started to return to

the rest of the platoon. As he walked up, one of the soldiers stared at him in shock.

"Willy?" he asked in a whisper. "Is that really you?"

"Sure, it's me. Why, what's wrong?"

The other soldier started crying. "I can't believe it, you're okay!"

"What's the big deal?" Willy asked in bewilderment. "We just went to plant land mines."

"Well, where's your coat? You're not wearing it."

"Yeah, I left it by the foxhole I was digging before."

"Well, Willy, you won't believe what happened. Go take a look over by that tree where you were digging that hole. Someone was practicing with live mortars, and by mistake he aimed them in the wrong direction. It landed in your foxhole and blew it up. When we found shreds of your winter coat there, we were sure you had been blown up. If you had been there, it would have been all over for you."

Once again, Hashem had watched over Willy, and had sent the sergeant to save him from certain death.

■ ■ ■

Once Willy's company was out in the fields, and the trucks were late in picking them up. When the trucks arrived, the men piled into the back of the truck, sitting on the built-in wooden benches.

One of the drivers asked Willy if he wanted to sit in the front, next to him. So Willy settled down in the comfortable seat, ready to enjoy the ride back to the barracks.

Just then, one of the sergeants came by. He took one look at Willy, noticed his rank, and decided that this simply wouldn't do. He walked right up to where Willy was sitting.

"Look," he pointed to the single stripe on Willy's sleeve. "You're a private. And you see these?" He pointed to his own sleeve, which had three stripes. "I'm a sergeant. That means that I sit here, and you go in the back."

Embarrassed, Willy had no choice but to get down from his seat and go in the back with the other soldiers. Not only that, but by the time he got there, every seat had been taken, and he had to stand.

The truck began moving along. Willy, who was standing up, had the best view of everyone in the truck. He suddenly noticed a small tornado coming right toward them.

"Hey!" he yelled to the driver. "There's a tornado up ahead!"

The driver looked around frantically. He finally spotted the tornado, directly ahead. In panic, he jerked the wheel of the truck, and the tires went off the road and into a ditch. The truck began to turn over. The men in the back had been alerted by Willy's warning, and they managed to jump clear in time.

When the truck finally came to a stop, the men ran forward to investigate. The driver was miraculously unhurt. But the sergeant who had taken Willy's seat had been killed in the crash.

■ ■ ■

In one area on the field, long-range missiles were shot up for testing. One day, Willy and his company were in an adjoining field, and they were watching the missiles going up in the air. At first they were enjoying the spectacle, hearing the sounds of the missiles being shot up and watching them move at terrifying speeds. In a moment, however, their excitement turned to terror: one of the missiles was coming down right at them!

The soldiers in the platoon began to scream and run. Actually, there was no way they would be able to avoid the explosion and the scraps of metal that would shoot out from the exploding missile. Still, they had to do something. So they all began to run.

After a few moments, Willy stopped short. *Be practical*, he said to himself. *There's no way I'll be able to outrun that thing. I had better make use of the time I have left.*

Willy began to say *Shema Yisrael*. He lifted his face to the sky and said, "Hashem, if You want me, I am ready to come to You." Willy continued to *daven*, and became so involved in what he was doing that he completely lost track of his surroundings. When he finally came back to himself, he noticed to his surprise that the day had passed. It was evening already. The missile must have landed long ago. Clearly, there had been no explosion! Willy thanked Hashem for his escape from death.

■ ■ ■

Aside from the two week yearly work details, there were meetings that Willy was required to attend. Usually, the meetings were held during the week, so Willy had no problem going. Sometimes, though, the meetings were scheduled on *yom tov*. At times like that, Willy would go to the sergeant major, a very accommodating Italian, and explain that since he had a holiday, he would need to be excused from the meeting.

"Come back to me tonight," the sergeant major would always tell him. "I'll let you know then." And when Willy came back that night, the sergeant major always gave him permission to miss the meeting.

This went on for a year. When the second year of scheduled meetings began, the sergeant major continued to go through the same procedure. Finally, Willy said to him, "You know, I've been with you for over a year. You know who I am. Who is it that you speak to before giving me permission to be excused from the meeting?"

"There's a Jewish sergeant in the company," the Italian explained. "I always ask him to make sure it's holiday time."

"Really?" Willy said in surprise. "I didn't know that there was a Jewish sergeant. Who is it?"

"It's Sergeant Smothers*," the man told him.

"What!" Willy couldn't believe it. "That man's a Nazi, not a Jew! Why are you asking *him* about my religion?"

"No, no," the sergeant major insisted. "He really is a Jew. He even has one of those pictures from when he was little, with the long curls by his ears. Come with me, I'll introduce you to him."

In a few minutes, Willy was being introduced to Sergeant Smothers. "Show him the picture from when you were little," the Italian urged.

Smothers needed no second invitation. He proudly removed the picture from a drawer and showed it to Willy. Sure enough, there was a little Jewish boy, complete with long, curly *payos*.

After the sergeant major left, Willy said to Smothers, "You know, that picture doesn't look like you."

"My whole family was destroyed in the war," Smothers told him. "I'm the only one who survived."

"Do you know what I said when the sergeant major told me you were Jewish?" Willy said then. "I told him that you were a Nazi. I asked him why he was asking a Nazi about my religion. You certainly don't act like a Jew!"

"Well, I'm sorry," Smothers said stiffly. "I went through all those camps, and I just don't believe in G-d anymore."

"Can't you see what you're doing?" Willy asked him.

---

*Name is fictitious.

"You're finishing up the Nazis' job for them. Not only did they kill your parents, but they've also gotten you to give up your *Yiddishkeit*. You've accomplished everything the Nazis wanted!"

"You don't understand," Smothers began to mumble. "You can't understand what I went through . . ."

"Look," Willy interrupted. "Maybe you don't want to act like a Jew yourself. But look at how you've been treating me! Badly enough that I was sure you were a Nazi! What did that accomplish?"

"Well, I had to," Smothers said lamely. "If other people saw me helping you, they would say, 'Look, those Jews are just helping each other.'"

"Don't worry," Willy told him. "There's no way anyone can know you're Jewish. You even fooled me! Just look at how the Italian sergeant major is treating me—much more nicely than my fellow Jew!"

Sergeant Smothers was deeply shaken by Willy's words. He eventually had a complete change in attitude, and began going out of his way to help Willy—even after they left the army.

■ ■ ■

During the time that Willy was in upstate New York, the same sergeant major noticed that he had nothing to eat, since kosher food wasn't available in the field.

One day, he went over to Willy. "Look, you can't only eat vegetables. You're running up and down mountains all day. You need some good food to keep you going."

"I can't eat the regular food," Willy tried to explain. "It isn't kosher."

The sergeant major noticed that Willy was carrying around his own food supply.

"You drag that around with you every day?" he exclaimed, pointing to Willy's cans of tuna. "Forget all that! I'll buy you a steak with my own money if you can't eat the regular food!"

"Thanks," Willy said uncomfortably. "I really appreciate the offer, but I'm not allowed to eat that."

"Look," the sergeant major said finally. "There's got to be something I can do for you. At least I can keep you from carrying that package around with you the whole day. I'll keep it for you, and at meal times, I'll give it to you."

The sergeant major went over to the captain to explain to him what was going on. "Feit not only carries his own gear, but he has to bring his own food supply along, too. We're driving around in a jeep all day, while he's running and walking the entire time. Let's leave his food in the jeep, and we'll give it to him at meal time."

The rest of the platoon also benefited from this arrangement. Until then, they had no way of knowing when meal time was: when the trucks with the food managed to find the areas where the soldiers were located, they were finally allowed to eat. This way, when they saw the captain looking for Feit, the others knew that mealtime couldn't be far behind.

■ ■ ■

One episode that Willy was not personally involved in happened to three other soldiers who were stationed in a different unit. The three Jewish soldiers were *shomer Shabbos*, and they wanted to go home for *Shabbos*. Since they were far from New York, they would have to leave early on Friday in order to get there in time.

The lieutenant of their unit was unwilling to make any concessions for them. Instead, he decided to stretch out the

Friday detail, so they would have no way of making it in time for *Shabbos*.

The three men came over to the lieutenant and asked him to let them out early.

"I'm the one in charge here," he said gruffly. "Don't you tell me what to do!"

And all their pleas fell on deaf ears.

Sure enough, by the time the lieutenant let them leave to the city, it was very late. Eventually, they realized that there was no way they would make it before sundown. A few minutes before candle-lighting time, they asked the truck driver to stop at a motel, and the three of them got out.

The lieutenant, who had also come along on the truck, couldn't understand what was happening. "Where are you going? Why are you getting off the truck?"

"It's almost our Sabbath," one of the men replied, "and we're not allowed to travel any further."

"I order you to get back on this truck!" the lieutenant yelled.

"I'm sorry, but we can't travel on our Sabbath. We told you that we wouldn't be able to. We'll be stopping here."

And with that, the three of them turned and went into the motel.

On Sunday morning, the three soldiers returned to the base and found the lieutenant waiting for them.

"You three are going to be court-martialed!" he told them furiously. "You deliberately disobeyed my orders!"

The three men weren't worried, however. They knew that they had the right to keep their Sabbath, and that it was the lieutenant who was in the wrong. They decided to hire a private lawyer to take charge of their case.

When the case came up for trial, their lawyer threatened to bring the issue to the attention of the public. He told the court that he would tell the newspapers and radio about what had happened. Things reached the point where Governor Rockefeller heard about what was going on. He immediately got in touch with the army.

"Tell the lieutenant to drop this case fast," he commanded them. "We don't need a public embarrassment now!"

The lieutenant immediately dropped the charges, and the three men were also willing to let it go. However, it was clear that they wouldn't be able to stay in their unit.

The commanding general of the New York Guard called a meeting of his fellow officers and asked if anyone had any experience in handling this sort of situation.

"I do," one of the captains there said. "There is a religious Jew in my unit, and we get on very well together."

"How do you manage that?" the general asked.

"It's simple," the captain replied. "I told him, 'Whatever you have to do, do quietly, and don't tell me anything about it.'"

The following day, the three men joined up with Willy. The captain took Willy to the side and said, "Just tell them the rules: whatever they need to do, they can do. I just don't want to hear anything about it."

■ ■ ■

In time, Willy finished his army requirement, and life went back to normal. He married, pursued a livelihood and supported his family. The army years began to fade as day-to-day living took over.

Still, in retrospect, one lesson Zev gained from his experiences in the army was how to live as a Torah Jew—no matter what the circumstances.

2
FAITH AND DIVINE PROVIDENCE

Entebbe Alive
■ ■ ■
Remember, it's Shabbos!
■ ■ ■
Mitzvah Protection
■ ■ ■
In the Numbers
■ ■ ■
A Gift of Life
■ ■ ■
Long-Deferred Appreciation
■ ■ ■
A Blessing Come True
■ ■ ■
Frostbite
■ ■ ■
Journey to Health
■ ■ ■
Care for My Children
■ ■ ■
Catalyst for a Car
■ ■ ■
Lost and Found
■ ■ ■
Saved by the Enemy
■ ■ ■
A Mother's Kerchief
■ ■ ■

2
Faith and Divine Providence

ENTEBBE ALIVE

The date was Sunday, June 27, 1976. Mr. Gilbert Weill, an Orthodox Jew, was returning from *Eretz Yisrael* to his home in Antwerp, Belgium. The flight he and his wife were booked on was due to leave early that morning. But upon arrival at the airport, they were told that the flight was delayed. The airline offered them the option of either waiting for their regular flight, or taking a different Air France flight, which had a stopover in Athens.

Mr. Weill and his wife were eager to return home as soon as possible. And so they decided to take Air France Flight 139. They had no way of knowing that they would arrive home much later than they had imagined.

The plane departed Ben Gurion airport and landed in Athens right on time. Four travelers boarded the plane at the Athens airport, ostensibly to travel on to Paris. Two of the passengers were men of Arabic origin. The other two were a man and woman of German origin, later identified as Gavriele Kroche Tiedemann, a well-known terrorist, and Wilferied Bose, a member of the Baader Meinhof-Urban guerrillas. One of the Arabs turned out to be a founder and planner of the terrorist group Popular Front for the Liberation of Palestine (PFLP).

Security was lax at the Athens airport due to a ground staff strike. And so the four passengers joined the flight without passing through metal detectors or any other routine checking. With everyone in his seat, Flight 139 departed for Paris.

Mr. Weill and his wife were seated in the front row of economy class, right next to the first class cabin. Around noontime, just a short while after takeoff, Mr. Weill was relaxing in his seat, glancing around the crowded plane. Suddenly he noticed an Arab running toward the first class cabin with what seemed to be a gun in his hand.

"Did I see that right?" Mr. Weill wondered. He rubbed his eyes in disbelief, unable to credit the reality of what he had seen.

A few seconds later, however, the other three passengers who had boarded in Athens also ran down the aisle and into the first class cabin. Within moments, the aisle was filled with confused and panicky passengers and stewards who were being chased out of the first class cabin and forced into the economy cabin. The frightened stewards tried to calm the even more hysterical passengers, who were demanding to know what was going on.

Suddenly the loudspeaker crackled to life, and a woman with a heavy German accent began to speak in English.

"This plane is now under the control of the Che Guevara group and the Gaza unit of the PFLP."

Pandemonium broke loose as the passengers began to realize the danger they were in. This malicious group of terrorists were well known for their cruelty and single-mindedness in achieving their goals. There was a very real concern that they would blow up the plane.

The two Arabs came back into the economy cabin.

"Everyone put their hands over their heads!" they barked.

The passengers immediately complied. The Arabs, holding guns and hand grenades, began searching each passenger individually. Passports were confiscated, and the Arabs demanded that any weapon, including all knives and forks, be handed over immediately. The procedure took several hours, during which time the plane continued to fly steadily, with no clue as to their destination.

At around three o'clock in the afternoon, the plane began to descend. After circling several times, the plane landed.

"We have landed in Benghazi, Libya," the leader of the terrorists declared.

The Arabs placed explosives near the doors while the plane was on the ground to prevent any intrusions. The doors were kept closed, and the passengers were ordered to keep the window shades down.

Mr. Weill risked a small peek out the window. The surrounding airfield was filled with soldiers, who were patrolling around the whole area.

After two hours, one woman, a British citizen who was pregnant, made a sudden announcement.

"I'm in labor! I must get off the plane!"

The passengers went into an uproar at the woman's announcement. Finally, the terrorists allowed a doctor on the plane, who examined the woman and confirmed that she was in labor. The woman was allowed off the plane and was eventually sent back to London. It was at this point that the first accounts of the hijacking were reported to British security.

Cans of Pepsi were passed out to all the passengers. Mr. Weill spoke quietly to his wife. "Perhaps we should save these for *Shabbos*, in case we're still captives then."

The thought of still being captive on *Shabbos*, six days away, was a daunting one. But Mrs. Weill agreed with her husband, and they put the cans of soda away.

The plane remained where it was for six more hours. At about seven o'clock, a cold meal was served; Mr. and Mrs. Weill, in keeping with their strict standards of *kashrus*, were only able to eat the vegetables. At ten o'clock, the plane began to taxi down the runway and took off.

After they were in the air for around an hour, one of the terrorists announced that they were flying to Uganda. Mr. Weill thought grimly that a world tour was not what he had had in mind when he had started on this trip—and certainly not Uganda. But his personal preferences notwithstanding, the plane continued to its destination, finally landing at 4:00 AM.

The passengers peeked out the windows of the plane. The most noticeable landmark was Lake Victoria, which confirmed to the more knowledgeable passengers that they were indeed in Uganda. Soldiers surrounded the plane outside.

Finally, the terrorists announced, "We have landed in Uganda." The passengers applauded. After the noise had died down, the announcement continued, "President Marshal Idi Amin Dada will be coming to greet us."

At this point, it was already morning, and Mr. Weill wanted to *daven Shacharis*. Since his own *tallis* and *tefillin* were packed in his luggage, he asked another Orthodox man on the flight, an American, to lend him his. Mr. Weill was unwilling to compromise his principles, despite the tense situation he was in. And so he donned the *tallis* and *tefillin* in full view of the passengers and terrorists and began to *daven*. Incredibly enough, the terrorists did not say a word to him.

When he was finished *davening*, Mr. Weill began to walk down the aisle of the plane, asking other Jewish passengers if they were interested in putting on the *tefillin*. Surprisingly, several people agreed, and Mr. Weill assisted them in putting on the *tefillin*.

In the early afternoon, the terrorists suddenly ordered everyone to stand up and get ready to leave the plane. The passengers slowly disembarked and were directed by several soldiers into an old, abandoned terminal. More soldiers lined the path into the terminal, keeping close guard on the hostages. As the passengers got off the plane, President Idi Amin Dada, otherwise known as "Big Daddy" due to his heavy physique, ran forward to greet the terrorists.

The passengers were led into a dusty lounge. "Big Daddy" entered a short while later. He was in a good mood, laughing and shaking hands with the frightened hostages.

"Welcome to Entebbe!" he declared. "We will do our utmost to ensure that your stay here in Uganda is as comfortable as possible." Idi Amin stressed that he would do as much as possible to help the passengers, and that he cared more about their welfare than Israel did. Clearly, "Big Daddy" was trying to portray himself as a good-hearted negotiator between Israel and the terrorists, as opposed to being affiliated with the terrorists.

Idi Amin then went on to explain the terrorists' demands. "Negotiations are being made with Israel for the release of forty-nine terrorists in exchange for the hostages. If these demands are not met, the hostages will be killed."

To Mr. Weill's astonishment, several passengers applauded after this announcement.

"What are you so happy about?" he hissed to a fellow traveler.

"Idi Amin loves honor," the man explained softly. "And there's no telling what mood he'll be in from one moment to the next. It's best to humor him."

A different passenger found this out the hard way. When he addressed Idi Amin simply as "Mr. President," Big Daddy responded angrily, "I am His Excellency Al-Hajji, Field Marshal Dr. Idi Amin Dada, holder of the British Victoria Cross, DSO MC and appointed by G-d Almighty to be your savior!"

A few hours went by. As night began to fall, soldiers brought mattresses into the lounge. These mattresses were new, with the paper wrappings still attached. The passengers were not allowed to remove the wrappings, and so the crackling of the paper kept many of them up all night.

Monday eventually arrived. Meals were served; Mr. and Mrs. Weill could only eat some bananas and vegetables. Afterwards, with breakfast over, the passengers found that time hung heavy on their hands. They had nothing to do but think about the situation they were in.

Suddenly an elderly woman, a concentration camp survivor, began screaming hysterically, as her current fright and past memories conspired to erode her fragile calm. Until now, morale had been high, but this incident served to underscore the true helplessness of their situation. The passengers grew silent as they realized that there was nothing they could do but wait and hope for the best.

On Tuesday, the Air France crew asked if more room could be arranged for the hostages, since the lounge was extremely crowded. The terrorists ordered soldiers to break through the wall of the lounge to open up an adjoining room. As the soldiers worked, Mr. Weill noticed the terrorists thumbing through the passports they had confiscated.

When the soldiers had broken a small hole through the wall, the terrorists ordered them to stop. They then began to call out the names of all the people who had been traveling with Israeli passports. A chill went through Mr. Weill as he observed the scene. He himself had been fortunate enough not to experience the horrors of World War II. But as he watched the terrorists choose people to send into the other lounge, he suddenly understood the true meaning of a "*selekzia.*" The people who were selected began to cry as a feeling of impending execution permeated the room.

Those who had had their names called out were told to collect their belongings and enter the other room. The small hole the soldiers had broken in the wall was too small to accommodate an adult, and so each person had to bend down and crawl into the small space.

After a few moments, Mr. Weill heard his own name called, despite the fact that he and his wife did not have Israeli passports. Mr. Weill tried to mingle with some passengers on the other side of the lounge to avoid going into the small room, but the German woman came over to him and, with her gun pointed straight at him, made it clear that she expected Mr. Weill and his wife to obey her directive.

As Mr. Weill came into the small room, he discovered that besides the Israelis, several hostages from each nationality had been ordered to enter the room, including the crew from the Air France flight.

The room was cramped and full of boxes, which, the terrorists warned them, contained explosives. One terrorist was stationed inside the room to watch the terrified hostages. He turned out to be mean and quick-tempered: when one man asked for a pillow for his baby, he was rewarded instead with a violent blow from the butt of the terrorist's gun.

Wednesday came with no hint of respite from their desperate situation. Mr. Weill was now afraid to do anything that would anger the terrorists; although he did *daven*, he did not put on his *tefillin*.

At eleven-thirty that morning, "Big Daddy" arrived. As he stooped to enter their tiny lounge, the passengers grew rigid in fear. Fortunately, however, his first word was an affable, "*Shalom!*" The relieved passengers applauded their approval.

"I have no personal grudge against you," Idi Amin declared. "Our sole grievance is with the Israeli government. If they do not accede with the terrorists' demands, it simply means that Israel does not care about your fate."

"If you really care about us, why don't you overpower the terrorists and release us?" one passenger demanded.

"Oh, I don't dare to do that. Why, if the terrorists feel that their aim is being thwarted, they could easily blow up the whole building!"

Idi Amin left on that note.

The rest of the day dragged by. Later, the hostages in the small lounge discovered that the passengers in the outer lounge had been released and taken to the French consulate, where they eventually continued on to Paris.

Thursday brought the return of Idi Amin, who announced that Israel had not yet consented to the terrorists' demands. The deadline had been set for Sunday at midday.

The hostages were unnerved by this announcement. An air of sadness and depression settled heavily on the small lounge.

In the afternoon, the terrorists came in with a list of

names. Each person had to respond to his name; after each response, the terrorist checked off that name. Anyone who was slow to respond was rewarded with sharp slaps and threats. After the checklist was complete, the hostages were brought back into the now-empty main lounge.

At six o'clock, a stunning announcement was made: Israel had accepted the terrorists' demands! The hostages began to hug and kiss one another in delight and gratitude. A palpable relief took the place of the earlier depression.

The French captain explained that it would take at least eight hours for a plane to come and pick them up. And so the countdown began, with the hostages joyously and impatiently counting off the hours to freedom.

But the hours passed, and no one came.

Friday dawned with no plane and no news. The Weills had barely eaten anything the entire week. Even their water ration was unusable; it was completely infested with flies.

Shabbos was quickly approaching, and Mr. Weill decided to do whatever he could to prepare for the holy day. He and his wife tidied around their mattresses and washed up. Other passengers, observing their efforts, began to join in.

There were no *Shabbos* candles available, but Mrs. Weill and another woman lit matches as a remembrance of the candle lighting*. The women watched silently as the matches burned down, until the flames were only a memory.

Mr. Weill *davened Kabbolas Shabbos* and *Maariv*, and then made *Kiddush* on some rolls that he had saved.

Mr. and Mrs. Weill sat down to their innovative *Shabbos* meal: a can of Pepsi, one of the cans that they had saved from the first day of their imprisonment. Mr. Weill was intrigued to see that many of the others—most of whom were not

---

*A berachah is not said in this situation.

religious—were having their own *Shabbos* meals and singing *zemiros*. The *kedushas Shabbos* was palpable, even in those circumstances.

One passenger came over to the Weills with a piece of chicken. "Look, all you've had to eat was a little bit of bread. Why don't you take this?" he urged.

The Weills politely declined the offer.

Later that evening, Idi Amin came by. "Israel has declined our offer," he said angrily. "You are all to write a telegram, stating that if no concessions have been made by Sunday noontime, we will begin killing one hostage every hour."

The day, which had begun with hope, thus ended in silence and despair.

Mr. Weill awoke early the following morning, only to discover that all the other passengers had been up all night in tremendous pain. Apparently, the chicken had been contaminated, and everyone who had eaten the food had suffered from food poisoning. Only the religious Jews, who had refrained from eating it due to their strict *kashrus* standards, had been spared.

For *Shabbos* lunch, Mr. and Mrs. Weill drank a little more of their first can of soda, which they had saved from the night before.

The day passed with no further news.

Motzei Shabbos, Mr. Weill *davened Maariv* and made *Havdalah* on a cup of tea. Then something interesting happened. Throughout that whole trying week, the passengers had kept to themselves, without offering to share their food. Tonight, however, with the deadline looming closer, the hostages began to pass around their supplies. The Weills were thus able to feast on a kosher chocolate bar for *Melaveh Malka*.

The night was getting late, and Mr. Weill began to prepare for bed. Right after he said *Krias Shema*, he noticed the terrorist on guard get up and leave the room. Nothing unusual in that. But then Mr. Weill's gaze drifted to the German terrorist. And as he watched, she lifted her machine gun, aimed outside the terminal, and began shooting.

What was happening?

Moments before, a crew of four Hercules aircraft had silently glided over Lake Victoria and dropped onto the runway. Brigadier General Dan Shomron led his men down the ramp of the leading airplane. One group, led by Lieutenant Colonel Yonni Netanyahu, took care of the Ugandans who were guarding the control tower, while the other taskforce sprinted toward the passenger building.

One German terrorist was standing guard outside, unaware of the men coming up behind him. The sound of gunfire broke the silence as one soldier took aim at him and fired.

The German woman was next. A quick glance at the soldiers outside made it clear that her cause was lost. Realizing that her end was near, she was nevertheless determined to get one religious Jew. She quickly armed her grenade, aimed it carefully, and tossed it inside the terminal, moments before the Israeli soldier raised his submachine gun and emptied his entire clip at her.

Mr. Weill had seen the flashes coming from the German terrorist's gun. But he didn't wait to watch. He quickly took his wife, and the two of them hid behind a wall. Seconds after they moved, the German woman's grenade landed on their mattresses and exploded.

The Israelis burst into the terminal. "Lie down!" they

shouted in Hebrew. "On the floor! Down!" The hostages froze in their places, stretched out motionless. Two Palestinian terrorists were still in the lounge. They both began to open fire, and the Israelis returned a storm of bullets in their direction.

Minutes later, the shooting stopped. The Israelis began to move cautiously around the room, checking that there were no more terrorists hiding among the hostages. They then directed the hostages to leave the terminal and enter a waiting car, which drove them to the army aircraft. The passengers could still hear sounds of gunfire in the distance; the car drove without lights, for they were not yet out of danger.

The passengers boarded the plane quietly. Most were dazed at the sudden turn of events. It was hard to believe that their ordeal was over, that they were actually on their way to freedom.

The Israelis, however, were worried. Rain had been falling that night, and it was quite possible that the plane would not be able to take off. The pilot cautiously started the plane rolling, hoping to attain the speed needed for takeoff. The darkened plane moved silently down the runway, while the pilot held his breath. Would they make it?

Yes! The plane was in the air, and the soldiers breathed a sigh of relief. They were finally on their way.

Now the Israelis had another concern. The plane had to land and refuel en-route, but only Kenya was willing to allow the Israelis to land. Kenya, however, was far beyond the usual flying range on the amount of fuel that they had; under normal circumstances, they would never have been able to make it there. Somehow, the plane managed to get to Kenya with only seven minutes of flying time left.

The plane finally landed in Israel. The tired hostages

filed out of the plane, only to discover that practically all of Israel was there to greet them. The *simcha* of that moment was completely indescribable. Mr. Weill himself had stayed strong and calm throughout the ordeal; upon his arrival in Israel, however, he burst into tears of gratitude.

Shortly after his arrival in Israel, Mr. Weill suddenly remembered a dream that he had had in Entebbe.

It had happened on Tuesday night. That was the day the German terrorist had forced Mr. Weill to enter the small lounge, and the group of selected passengers had been understandably fearful.

That night, Mr. Weill's father, who had passed away a few years before, came to him in a dream. "Don't worry," his father reassured him. "Both you and your wife will leave Entebbe unharmed."

As he recalled the dream, Mr. Weill was overcome with the realization of the many miracles he had been privileged to witness[*]:

- The guard left the room seconds before the Israelis arrived. If the guard had been there then, he would undoubtedly have opened fire on the hostages.
- The Weills moved away from their mattresses seconds before the German's grenade landed where they had been and exploded.
- An Air France steward later told Mr. Weill that one of the terrorists had been ready to throw his grenade at the hostages. The steward shouted at him in French, "Throw it out!" Remarkably, although the man did not know French, he listened to her and threw the grenade out the window.

---

[*] *A few years after this event, Iran took some Americans hostage. The Americans had their ships in position to rescue the hostages, but the rescue was unsuccessful. Man's plans can only come to fruition if it is the will of Hashem.*

- The plane took off without any problems despite the weather conditions, which the pilot later admitted was an absolute miracle.
- The plane managed to make it to Israel despite a lack of fuel.

During the first *Rosh Hashana* and *Yom Kippur* after the event, Mr. Weill was overcome by the words of *Unesane Tokef*. "Who will live and who will die . . . who will be tranquil and who will be tormented . . . " The hijacking had brought that concept forcibly home to him.

Mr. Weill has never forgotten to be grateful. There was one soldier who had been shot and paralyzed during the rescue in Entebbe. Mr. Weill always arranges to have him brought to Antwerp for the Weill family's *bar-mitzvahs* and *chasunahs*. This soldier once told Mr. Weill, "Many have forgotten me, but I see that you still have *hakoras hatov* for what I did for you."

What happened to the second can of Pepsi? Mr. and Mrs. Weill shared it on their first *Shabbos* back in Antwerp. And every year, the Weills make a feast of thanks for the miracle that Hashem bestowed upon them.

REMEMBER, IT'S SHABBOS!

Chazal state, "The world was created for the sake of Yisrael." (Rashi, Bereishis 1:1) Hashem created the world for Bnei Yisrael, and all world events transpire solely for their benefit. The following historical incident, as told by Rabbi Dovid Hersh Mayer, the menahel of Yeshivas Bais Binyomin of Stamford, Connecticut, is a case in point.

In 1932, America was still in the throes of the Great Depression. Incumbent president Herbert Hoover ran for a second term against Franklin Roosevelt, who promised to institute many economic reforms in an effort to bring the United States out of the financial doldrums. Among his proposed reforms was a promise to the labor unions that he would institute a five-day work week.

Roosevelt won the presidential elections and began his four terms in office in 1933. Soon after his inauguration, he began instituting his economic reforms, including the five-day work week. The workers were happy, the unions were pleased, and the Jews were jubilant. At last, the terrible trials of working on *Shabbos* would be taken away!

Until Roosevelt's revolutionary proposal, the six-day work week, from Monday through Saturday, was an accepted institution in America. This put an incredible strain on the immigrants of Europe who came to America to make a living for their families, only to find that the security of their jobs was dependent on their willingness to work on *Shabbos*.

Many otherwise upright Jews, who would have preferred to remain *shomer Shabbos*, found themselves unable to make a living and eventually succumbed to the *nisayon*. In fact, there was an established prayer, composed for a woman to recite after lighting the *Shabbos* candles on behalf of her husband who was forced to work on *Shabbos*. Upon retirement, many men would make a *kiddush* in *shul* to celebrate their return to *shemiras Shabbos*. It seemed to be an unhappy yet unavoidable circumstance to life in America.

Roosevelt's new law was the beginning of a tremendous

change in the American workplace. While the complete elimination of the *nisayon* of *shemiras Shabbos* on a national basis did not occur until many years later, Roosevelt's reforms cleared the way for the future, when refugees from war-torn Europe streamed into the United States. Those Jews who had survived the horrors of the Holocaust were now spared, to some degree, the terrible trial of *shemiras Shabbos* in order to make a living. Indeed, Hashem orchestrates world affairs for the sake of His people, Yisrael!

■ ■ ■

R' Mayer was once privileged to meet one of those special Jews who had resisted the *nisayon* of working on *Shabbos* in the early decades of the twentieth century. In the mid-1960's, on one of R' Mayer's many visits to his mother in Seagate, New York, he noticed a elderly Jew playing the fiddle. Intrigued by the old man's liveliness, he asked his mother about the old fiddler.

"Oh, that's R' David," R' Mayer's mother said with a smile. "He's already in his nineties, and he still loves playing his fiddle."

On his subsequent visits, R' Mayer struck up an acquaintance with the elderly man. R' David was a cheerful, good-natured person with a vast amount of experience and wisdom. He often regaled R' Mayer with stories from his younger days in turn-of-the-century America.

Once, while R' David was regaling R' Mayer with tales of his experience, the old fiddler's children and grandchildren came to visit. R' Mayer withdrew quietly to one side and watched R' David's face glow with happiness and pride as he spoke with his children. R' Mayer was intrigued to note that all of R' David's children and grandchildren were obviously observant, prestigious Jews. How could a man who had grown up in America at the turn of the twentieth century, at a time when the United States was considered to be a *treife medinah*, a non-kosher country, merit to have such wonderful, religious children?

On his next visit to Seagate, R' Mayer delicately brought up the subject. R' David smiled broadly and said, "There's a story behind that. Listen and I'll tell you all about it.

"Today, I am free to while away the hours playing the fiddle. But when I was young like you, I spent all my time trying to make a living and put a little food on the table.

"I can't begin to explain the strain of trying to be *shomer Torah* and *mitzvos* when one simply cannot find a job that does not require working on *Shabbos*. Many Jews, who were otherwise observant, found themselves forced to work on *Shabbos*. These same Jews felt so guilty over what they were doing that they applied tremendous peer pressure on their friends, urging them to join them in desecrating *Shabbos*. I suppose their consciences wouldn't let them rest at seeing other Jews who were able to withstand the *nisayon*.

"Well, the same thing happened to me. I was working at a factory and bringing home pennies. My friends told me I was crazy and that I would have to work on *Shabbos* to support my family, whether I liked it or not. I resisted this suggestion, but it became more and more difficult as I watched my family go hungry.

"The day came when there was literally nothing to eat in the house. My resolve weakened, and I gave in. I gave up my job and found another, better-paying job in a sewing factory where I would have to work on *Shabbos*.

"When the first *Shabbos* on my new job arrived, I awakened early to attend the first *minyan* in *shul*. After the *davening*, I slowly walked in the direction of the factory, crying as I went. This would be the first time I desecrated the

Shabbos! I couldn't bear the thought of it."

R' David paused and smiled, his eyes distant with memory. "But you see, Hashem was watching over me. He saved me from being *mechallel Shabbos.*"

"What happened?" R' Mayer asked, spellbound.

"I arrived at the factory and sat down at my sewing machine to begin working. My eyes must have been too clouded with tears to see very well, for when I began to feed the material under the needle, my finger got caught there instead. I literally 'sewed' my finger with the needle. The bleeding couldn't be stopped, and I had to be taken to the hospital for stitches."

R' David held up his hand and showed R' Mayer the scars that still remained on his finger. "After that, I never even entertained the thought of working on *Shabbos* again. My injured finger always served as a reminder of how Hashem had saved me from *chillul Shabbos* and gave me the strength to resist all future pressure.

"So you see, my friend, I was successful in defying the *nisayon* of working on *Shabbos* at a time when many others could not resist. I have always felt that Hashem chose to bless me with such good children in the *zechus* of my *Shemiras Shabbos.*"

MITZVAH PROTECTION

Besides the reward for their performance, mitzvos offer protection to those who are involved with them. (Shabbos 130a)

In the 1980's, the Allen Rothenberg law offices was one of the biggest *shomer Shabbos* law offices in Pennsylvania. When David Chaim Novitsky graduated from law school in 1986, it was natural for him to seek a job with the Allen Rothenberg law firm.

That May would mark the first anniversary of the bombing of the radical Move group in Philadelphia. One year before, the police had dropped a bomb on a fortified house which was barricaded by the members of Move. The purpose of the bomb had been to force the group out of the house. What the police had not known about, however, were the flammable explosives that were stored in the attic of the house. The bomb caused a fire to break out, which spread to all the houses in a two-block radius. By the time the dust had cleared, nearly two hundred people had become homeless, and the city had a number of lawsuits on its hands.

The Allen Rothenberg law firm picked up twelve of these clients. Since the houses were in a poorer section of the city, the lawyers did not expect to make much profit from these cases. It would, however, be a perfect first case for a new junior lawyer. And so the twelve cases wound up in the hands of David C. Novitsky, the newest member of the firm.

David was optimistic. After all, this was one of his first cases, and he was determined to give it his best shot and show the law firm what he could do. And so David worked tirelessly, putting in long hours and employing all the means at his disposal to see to it that his clients got the compensation that they deserved.

Ernest Bostic, age fifty, was one of David's clients. And Ernest Bostic was very eager to get his money. Bostic had a police record—he had already served time in jail—and he was used to getting what he wanted, when he wanted it. He had no time for long, drawn-out lawsuits. David's long hours and verbose explanations did not placate him in the least.

Before long, Bostic was a weekly fixture at the law firm. "What's taking so long?" he would demand of his hardworking lawyer.

"We're dealing with the city, Mr. Bostic," David would explain. "Everything takes a long time when you deal with the city. Why, even after the lawsuit is settled, it will still be a while before you get your money. Please, just be patient."

But Ernest Bostic was not convinced. He simply could not understand how the case could be taking so long. Eventually, he decided that it was David Chaim Novitsky who was holding out on him.

One night, after an exhausting day at the law firm, David had a horrifying dream. He dreamed that he was in his office when a man suddenly came up to him, pulled out a gun and shot him.

David woke up in a panic. His heart was pounding and his head was whirling. Should he disregard the dream? Did it signify anything? After a restless night, David finally decided that it wouldn't hurt to take some precautions.

David's precautions took the form of added protection—in the shape of *tzitzis*. David resolved to wear his *tzitzis* at all times. After all, if anything could protect him, *tzitzis* certainly would.

A few days after his dream, David was standing in his office at the law firm when Ernest Bostic stopped by for his weekly visit. David drew a deep breath, intending to placate him with his usual speech about being patient. But Bostic didn't give him a chance. Bostic had convinced himself that the long delay was all David's fault, and he had come prepared to deal with that. Before David could get a word out, Bostic pulled a gun out of his pocket and pointed it straight at him.

David turned instinctively and began to run into his boss's office. Bostic shot six bullets at David's back, but David managed to keep on running until he got into the office, where he collapsed.

Bostic ran for his life. The law offices were on the ninth floor, and there was no time to wait for an elevator, so Bostic took the stairs, leaping down them two at a time. Even a twisted ankle that he sustained on landing didn't slow him down. Ignoring the agonizing pain, Bostic managed to leave the building and head for the central bus station.

Back at the law firm, an ambulance arrived in record time and took David to Jefferson Medical College hospital, two blocks away. One of the top professors was available, and he whisked David straight into surgery. David's family was notified, and they quickly headed for the hospital, where they were informed that the operation was still in progress.

David's parents paced the waiting room, with prayers on their lips and entreaties in their hearts. Finally, the door to the operating room swung open, and the professor emerged.

He looked from one member of the family to the other. "It's simply a miracle," he said finally. "I've never seen anything like it."

"What happened?" David's mother whispered.

"I simply can't believe it," the professor said again. "Every single bullet was just a fraction of an inch away from hitting a vital organ.

"But I must caution you. We've only found five bullets so far. There is a sixth one that is still unaccounted for. He won't be out of danger until—"

The door to the operating room swung open again, and

the professor's assistant ran out. "We found the sixth bullet! It was in his arm!"

The professor smiled at David's parents. "Well, I guess we've found all the bullets. I'll go finish up the operation. It looks like your son will be all right."

"*Baruch Hashem*," David's father whispered.

The family stood there, tears rolling down their cheeks, as they thanked Hashem for His great *chesed*. "Give thanks to Hashem for He is good, for His kindness endures forever!"

Meanwhile, back at police headquarters, a search was underway for Ernest Bostic. As David had been carried into the ambulance for his trip to the hospital, a police officer had asked him if he knew who had shot him. David had managed to name his assailant before losing consciousness. Now the police had an all-points bulletin out for Ernest Bostic. But Bostic had already made it to the bus station before the alarm went out, and by the time the police started their search, he was already out of Philadelphia and heading to Detroit.

Bostic arrived in Detroit, penniless and in pain. He entered a mission, hoping to spend the night there. But the mission's policy was to impound any weapons that their guests might be carrying. "You'll get it back when you leave," he was told.

Bostic tried to rest, but the pain in his leg was worsening, and he needed medical attention. He headed for the nearest hospital emergency room.

The emergency room staff asked him where he was from as part of their routine questions. "Pennsylvania," was his initial reply. But then his fear got the better of him, and before he knew it, he was blurting out the whole story.

"I come from Philadelphia, and I just killed my lawyer!"

The startled nurse immediately called hospital security. The security guard spoke to Bostic, then called the police and related the story to them. The Detroit police in turn checked the national network and discovered that Bostic was wanted in Pennsylvania. He was immediately arrested and brought back to Philadelphia, where he was tried and sentenced to jail for his crime.

But to David Chaim Novitsky, the lesson was clear. He recalled the dream that he had had just a few nights before the shooting. And he knew, without a doubt, that it was his *tzitzis* which had guided each bullet so it would miss every vital organ—and spare his life.

■ ■ ■

Zev Kurtzman was born and raised in Scotland. For as long as he could remember, his dream was to move to Eretz Yisrael and live a life of Torah.

As soon as he was old enough, Zev left the land of his birth and settled in Eretz Yisrael. In the all-encompassing Torah environment of the Holy Land, Zev found his commitment to Torah growing with each passing day.

In the late 1950s Zev was called for army duty. He found himself in a very different environment from what he had become accustomed to in the religous *yishuv*. Still, he was determined to remain strong in his commitment to Torah and *mitzvos*.

One day Zev was surveying some abandoned Arab territory. As he walked across the field, his foot triggered a mine that had been laid in the ground. Zev tried to escape, but before he managed to move, the mine blew up.

Zev was completely covered with scrap metal. It was

clearly a miracle that he was alive. As the doctors worked on him, they noticed that the area of his body covered by his *tzitzis* did not have any cuts from the shrapnel. The *tzitzis* had taken the brunt of the explosion.

Zev clearly understood that his *tzitzis* had protected him from certain death and allowed him to continue in his life's work. And indeed, Zev's commitment to *Yiddishkeit* became even stronger. Eventually, he settled in Los Angeles, where he continued to spread Torah to scores of students.

IN THE NUMBERS

> *The ways of Hashem can be difficult for man to comprehend. Great is the man who nonetheless accepts Hashem's Divine providence, and has complete faith that all is for his good. The following personal story, told in Lakewood, New Jersey, in July 1995, by Tuvia Chaim Ariel of Yerushalayim, is a vivid lesson for all.*

Terel Howard was the quintessential, all-around American boy growing up in the Bronx. He was also Jewish, but that was entirely besides the point. He and his family were completely non-religious and were the only ones on the block without a trace of a European accent.

In 1954, Terel joined the United States Army. Shortly after his induction, he was stationed in Germany. Although the war had been over for nine years, Terel soon discovered that a strong undercurrent of anti-Semitism still lurked just beneath the surface. With his tall, blond looks, Terel hardly fit the German stereotype of a Jew, and many Germans felt free to vent their anti-Semitic hatred in his presence.

Disgusted and angered, Terel resolved to do whatever he could to stand between the Germans and his Jewish brothers. "Nothing's changed," he muttered to himself. "The world still hates the Jews. I'm going to move to Israel and help my people!"

As soon as Terel finished serving his term in the army, he fulfilled the promise he had made to himself and immigrated to Israel. He joined a kibbutz and spent his days doing manual labor. The hours were long and the work exhausting, but Terel was content to be among his fellow Jews.

With time, Terel developed a close friendship with David*, a carpenter on the kibbutz. Although David was a strong, powerful man with bulging muscles, Terel knew he was a Holocaust survivor who had nearly starved to death during World War II. During their frequent conversations, Terel often found himself staring at the four digits, 7401, that were tattooed on David's arm. Although he knew the numbers had something to do with the war, Terel could not help being fascinated by them, as those four numbers were the last four digits of his own American Social Security.

One day, he mustered enough courage to ask David about it. "I know you never talk about your past," he said hesitantly, "and I'm sorry for prying into your affairs. But I just have to ask you how you got those numbers on your arm."

David sat silently for a moment, staring at the four small digits, 7401, that marked his arm forever. Then he looked up at Terel and said slowly, "Look, Terel. I like you very much, so I'm willing to tell you about it. But I don't want you to ever ask me again."

---

* Name is fictitious.

Terel nodded mutely, afraid to even speak. After another long moment, David continued in a faraway, emotion-filled voice. "The Germans lined us up, one after another. I stood in line with my parents, my brothers and my sisters. They branded our arms in numerical order and then sent us away to die."

David paused. His eyes were filled with tears. "They killed all of them," he said softly. "I alone from my family escaped and came to Palestine. I am all alone now, except for my friends. I consider you a friend, Terel, and that's why I've told you all this, but I won't speak about it again. It hurts too much to remember."

Terel silently clasped David's hand, too moved to say anything. The two of them never spoke about the incident again.

With time, Terel moved away from the kibbutz and joined another one in a different part of the country. He was working as a heavy machinery operator when a terrible accident occurred and he lost his leg. Despite this loss, Terel lost none of his unshakable spirit and determined to find another way to make a livelihood. He became a tour guide and was soon famous as the only one-legged tour guide in Israel.

One day, Terel was assigned to pick up a tourist at the airport and drive him to the Hilton Hotel in Yerushalayim. Terel drove to the airport and met his passenger, a rich, well-dressed American with heavy gold cufflinks and a long, evil-smelling Cuban cigar. The man settled himself comfortably in the passenger seat of Terel's car and spoke expansively about his wealth and his business. Terel was frankly disgusted by the man's pompous attitude, but he contained himself and concentrated on his driving. He wasn't being paid to like his clients. A job was a job, after all.

As they neared Yerushalayim, the tourist suddenly stopped talking. Terel glanced at him curiously and saw that the man was studying him closely.

"Can you pull over to the side for a minute?" the man asked.

Puzzled, Terel did as the man asked. He pulled over to the side of the road and stopped the engine.

"Yes?" he said with stiff politeness.

"I can tell you don't like me," the rich American said after a moment.

Terel, taken aback by the man's perception, merely shrugged.

"Well, I want to tell you something," the tourist went on. "You may think I'm nothing but a rich, eccentric American Jew, but I've paid my dues." He pulled up the sleeve of his expensive jacket and showed Terel the last thing he would have expected to see on this man's arm: a blue tattoo of four numbers. This rich American had suffered through the Holocaust.

"I've paid my dues," the man repeated quietly. "Do you blame me for wanting to be comfortable in life, after what I suffered in Europe?"

Terel glanced at the four digits branded on the man's arm. Then he froze. The numbers were 7402, the next following number after 7401, the last four digits of his Social Security number!

After a minute, Terel managed to tear his eyes away from the tattoo and look the American tourist in the face. "Tell me," he managed to say. "Did you have a brother named David?"

The man stared at him for a moment. "David!" He exclaimed. "Yes. Yes, I did have a brother named David. He stood in line right in front of me as the Germans branded the numbers on our arms. He was killed in the war, along with the rest of my family. But—how did you know?"

Terel's heart was pounding so loudly he could barely hear what the man was saying. He swallowed several times before he was able to speak. "I—I think your brother is still alive," he finally said hoarsely. "I think I know where he is. I—I can you take to him right now, if you want."

"If I want?!" The American tourist stared at him. "If you think is David is still alive -- yes, take me to him, quickly!"

With trembling hands, Terel restarted the engine and made a U-turn on the highway. They sped down the road in the direction of the kibbutz where Terel had first worked when he immigrated to Israel. Terel glanced at his American tourist from time to time, but the man was rigid, staring out the window with unseeing eyes, lost in memory.

When they arrived, Terel drove straight to the carpentry shop, hoping that David would still be working there. He vaulted out of the car and hobbled inside the building, where the first person he saw was David himself.

David looked up from his work and smiled with pleasure at the sight of his old friend Terel. His smile vanished when he saw the stump of Terel's missing leg.

"It's all right," Terel said quickly. "I didn't come here for myself. David, you must come outside. I've brought someone for you to see. I—I think it's your brother."

David stared at him, shocked. "How—what—"

Terel quickly explained that he had always remembered the number branded on David's arm because it matched the last four digits of his Social Security number. "I picked up a tourist today at the airport, and his number is the one right after yours. He said he had a brother named David . . ."

Without another word, David brushed past Terel and went outside. The American tourist was standing there next to the car, his face a mixture of anticipation and trepidation. At the sight of the carpenter, the man took a hesitant step forward. "David . . .?"

The two brothers immediately recognized each other and fell into each other's arms, crying uncontrollably out of pain and joy at finally being reunited with each other.

Terel couldn't watch the emotion-laden meeting. He quietly removed his former client's luggage from the car trunk and drove away. But when he reached the entrance of the kibbutz, he realized that his eyes were too blurred to see the road properly. He pulled the car to the side and started to cry, overwhelmed by the incredible miracle he had just witnessed. It was a long, long time before Terel was able to pull himself together and drive away.

This incident had such a great impact on Terel that he began to re-evaluate his life. With time, he became a true *baal teshuvah*.

Today, Terel is known as Tuvia Chaim Ariel. He is married, has a family of five and owns a bookstore on Agrippas Street in Yerushalayim. Although he is nearly sixty, he still devotes his life to the same caring and love for his fellow Jews that had prompted him as a young, irreligious American to move to Eretz Yisrael.

Tuvia has dedicated himself to seeking ways to ease the plight of other Jews with similar disabilities to his own. He founded the Jerusalem Institute for Rehabilitation to provide assistance and service for the estimated 25,000 amputees living in Israel.

Tuvia himself has done extensive research and has acquired a prosthetic leg made of materials developed for the U.S. space program. With this new, highly developed leg, Tuvia can run after his children as well as any other father blessed with his own limbs. He hopes to eventually be able to provide similar prosthetics for others. With this end in mind, he often travels all over the world to bring the best doctors in the field to Eretz Yisrael to train Israeli technicians in the latest techniques for producing and repairing artificial limbs.

Occasionally, magazines and newspapers publish articles about Tuvia's work and the Institute. Soon after an article had been written in a local paper, Tuvia received a phone call from a distressed mother.

"My Udi is only eight years old," the woman said tearfully. "He was born with a disease and we had to have his foot amputated. Please, is there any way you could come to our home and give Udi some moral support?"

Tuvia was scheduled to fly that night to America, but he didn't hesitate. "I'll come over as soon as I can," he promised. He called up his travel agent and arranged for a new reservation on a flight the following week.

That night, Tuvia arrived in Udi's home and spoke with the eight-year-old boy. "You can have a normal life," he told Udi encouragingly. "You can be just like everyone else. You'll see!" He even danced with the boy on his artificial leg to show him that it would be possible for him to do everything any other boy his age could do.

When Tuvia went home that night, he was gratified to know that he had improved Udi's spirits and given the boy hope for the future. However, he worried about the tremendous expense involved in fitting Udi with a new foot. How could he possibly raise the money?

That *Motzei Shabbos*, Tuvia was home when the phone rang. A woman with an English accent asked if she could meet him. Tuvia arranged a meeting for the following morning.

"I saw the article in the paper about your work," the

woman explained the next morning. "I was very impressed. I had originally intended to donate a large sum of money to a certain *tzedakah*, but I have just found out that it is no longer needed. I would like to give the money to you instead. I am sure you will find a good use for it." With a warm smile, she handed Tuvia a check for ten thousand English pounds, which is the equivalent of approximately $16,000.

After the woman left, Tuvia sat looking at the check for some time, awed at the manifest *hashgachah pratis* that had enabled him to receive this money. If he hadn't postponed his flight to talk to Udi, he would not have been home when the woman called. To Tuvia, this was a clear indication of Hashem's intent that Udi be provided with the prosthetic foot he needed.

Today, Udi is able to run, jump and play with other boys his age, while Tuvia is continuing his vital work in helping his fellow Jews.

A GIFT OF LIFE

Everyone agrees that life is the most precious of all gifts. It is our responsiblity to utilize this gift for the sake of Hashem and His service. In the following story, related by R' Moshe Londinski, this point is brought to the fore.

In the year 1928, the entire Jewish world was horrified to hear that the saintly Chafetz Chaim, at the age of eighty-eight, was terribly ill. All around the globe, prayers streamed heavenward as *Klal Yisrael* begged Hashem to spare the

Chafetz Chaim and allow him to recuperate and receive a complete *refuah sheleimah*.

One young man of twenty-three, who lived next door to the Chafetz Chaim, was particularly distressed. Rav Moshe Londinski was the *rosh yeshivah* of *Yeshivas Radin*, and his son, R' Mordechai, had long since cherished the unique opportunity to attend the Chafetz Chaim and fulfill his every need. Indeed, the Chafetz Chaim had often entrusted R' Mordechai with many responsibilities for the community. Now, his beloved rebbe was close to death. How could *Klal Yisrael* survive without the Chafetz Chaim's sure, guiding hand?

One evening, R' Mordechai entered the *beis medrash* and spent the entire night engrossed in the recital of *Tehillim*, tears streaming down his cheeks as he fervently prayed to Hashem for the Chafetz Chaim's recovery. Morning dawned and found R' Mordechai still hunched over his *Tehillim* in the deserted *beis medrash*, immersed in earnest prayer.

R' Mordechai looked around and saw that the *beis medrash* was empty. He hesitated for a moment, then slowly approached the *aron kodesh*. He felt that he must do more than just *daven* for the Chafetz Chaim. Now, with nobody else to witness what he was about to do, he opened the *aron kodesh* and lovingly kissed the *sifrei Torah*.

"*Ribono shel Olam*," he whispered. "*Klal Yisrael* needs the Chafetz Chaim. I am hereby giving up five years of my life for the Chafetz Chaim so that he should have a speedy recovery."

Without another word, R' Mordechai closed the *aron kodesh* and returned to his seat. People would soon be coming into the *beis medrash* for *Shacharis*, and he did not want anyone to know what he had done.

Days later, the electrifying news raced through Radin.

The Chafetz Chaim was recuperating! The danger was past! Within a few weeks, the Chafetz Chaim had fully recovered and was once more involved in his work for the *klal*.

R' Mordechai happily looked forward to resuming his holy duties for the Chafetz Chaim, but a nagging thought troubled him. He had granted five years of his life to his beloved rebbe, but he was only a young man in his early twenties. What good could five of his years be for a *gadol* of the Chafetz Chaim's stature? Perhaps someone on a higher level would be required to donate years for the Chafetz Chaim.

On the other hand, if the value of the years would be measured by the level of the recipient, there would be no problem. R' Mordechai would have given his *rebbe* five years which the Chafetz Chaim could use at his own sublime level. But how could he possibly know which theory was correct?

After some deliberation, R' Mordechai decided to approach the Chafetz Chaim and ask him a "theoretical question" without explaining why he was interested in the answer. He waited until the Chafetz Chaim was officially well enough for visitors, then entered the *tzaddik's* home and asked for an audience.

As R' Mordechai approached the Chafetz Chaim's desk, the *gadol* looked at him with a steady gaze and said, "Mordche, you should know that your *tefillos* were accepted in Heaven."

At first, R' Mordechai assumed that the Chafetz Chaim referred to his prayers which, like those of all *Klal Yisrael*, had been dedicated to the *gadol's* recovery. But the Chafetz Chaim continued, "I will give you my word, Mordche, that in the *zechus* of what you have given me, you will live to be as old as I am now."

R' Mordechai stared at his rebbe in shock. How had the Chafetz Chaim known of the offer he had made to Hashem in the early morning hours at the *beis medrash* several weeks ago?

The Chafetz Chaim lived for five more fruitful years before his *petirah* in 1933 at the age of ninety-three. R' Mordechai Londinski never breathed a word in public about the incident that had taken place between him and his *rebbe*, although he did relate the story to his oldest son, R' Moshe.

In Sivan of 1995, when he had just turned eighty-nine, R' Mordechai was *niftar*. He was one year older than the Chafetz Chaim had been during his near-fatal illness.

At R' Mordechai's *levayah*, R' Moshe repeated his father's story for the first time, then added, "My father would have wanted this story to be told for only one reason: to show the world more of the holiness and *gadlus* of the Chafetz Chaim."

■ ■ ■

When R' Mordechai was suddenly *niftar*, early one Thursday afternoon, his oldest son R' Moshe was out of town on the west coast. The question then arose whether to make the *levayah* quickly and allow the *aron* to arrive in Eretz Yisrael before *Shabbos*.

This question was presented to Rav Shmuel Kamenetsky, *rosh yeshivah* of the Philadelphia Yeshivah. He replied that it would be better to wait and allow the eldest son to be present at his father's *levayah*.

After his son R' Moshe delivered his eulogy and revealed his father's story for the first time, R' Shmuel remarked, "Now I understand the *siyatah deshmayah* behind making that decision."

LONG-DEFERRED APPRECIATION

Appreciation has a prominent place in Torah life. Many people do offer thanks for a favor done for them. However, it is unusual to find someone who will still express appreciation for a kindness that was done generations before.

R' Gavriel Banok* had left America as a *bachur* and settled in Eretz Yisrael. Now, in the summer of 1995, he found himself back in the United States. Several of his family members had suffered from severe illnesses and the medical bills were more than the family could handle. R' Gavriel decided to travel to America and try to do some fundraising to cover the tremendous medical expenses. As a former American, he was able to relate to his prospective donors with a bit more ease than others who came from Eretz Yisrael.

Most of Brooklyn had emptied in the heat of mid-summer and fled to the cooler air of the Catskills. R' Gavriel went up to the mountains himself to visit several people. One of the names on his list was a family called Weinberg*. R' Gavriel did not know the Weinbergs personally, but he had been assured that they were a fine family well-known for their generosity.

R' Gavriel found his way to the Weinberg's bungalow with little trouble and knocked on the door. Mrs. Weinberg graciously invited him inside and offered him a cold drink as she and her husband listened to R' Gavriel's story.

As R' Gavriel explained the difficulties in which his family found themselves, he could see that the Weinbergs

---

*Names are fictitious

were very moved by his plight. After a moment, Mr. Weinberg pulled out his checkbook. He wrote busily for a moment before tearing out the check and handing it to R' Gavriel.

"Go with *hatzlachah*," he said warmly. "And may Hashem grant your entire family a *refuah sheleimah*."

R' Gavriel thanked the Weinbergs and left. Once he was outside, he glanced at the check. His eyes widened with disbelief as he stared at it more closely. He was used to the usual ten or eighteen dollar checks. Sometimes one person would give him "double *chai*" of thirty-six dollars. But this check was for eighteen *hundred* dollars! Why would the Weinbergs give so much money to a complete stranger?

Marvelling at the Weinbergs' generosity with *tzedakah*, R' Gavriel took stock of his situation. It was already Thursday night, and there were still a few people in the mountains that he wanted to see. It would probably be best to spend *Shabbos* in the area and return to the city on Sunday.

That *Shabbos* afternoon, R' Gavriel met the Weinberg family as they took a stroll just outside the bungalow colony. They greeted him warmly and introduced him to Mrs. Weinberg's father, Mr. Kleinman, who was spending *Shabbos* with them. As they walked and chatted, the Weinbergs eventually moved several paces ahead, leaving Mr. Kleinman and R' Gavriel to continue their conversation alone.

In the course of their discussion, R' Gavriel used a modern Hebrew expression. Mr. Kleinman stopped and regarded him with faint disapproval.

"Where are you from?" he asked.

"I'm from Eretz Yisrael," R' Gavriel replied. "I've lived there for over twenty years."

Mr. Kleinman shook his head. "Well, talk to me in Yiddish or Galicianish, but not in Hebrew."

"Certainly," said R' Gavriel quickly and politely. "If that's what you prefer." They walked a few more steps in silence before R' Gavriel added, "You are originally from Galicia, then? That's interesting, because my family is, too."

"Oh, really?" Mr. Kleinman stopped again, but this time his face registered interest. "Where in Galicia?"

R' Gavriel chuckled. "A small town called Pshevorske."

Mr. Kleinman's eyes lit up. "That's interesting. My family was from there, too!"

"That's incredible," R' Gavriel said with a laugh. "Two strangers meeting each other, from Pshevorske to the Catskills!"

"What did you say your last name was?"

"Banok," R' Gavriel replied.

Mr. Kleinman stared at him for a moment before he said, "Are you by any chance related to R' Alexander Banok?"

It was R' Gavriel's turn to look surprised. "Why, yes," he answered. "R' Alexander was my great-grandfather."

Mr. Kleinman gripped the younger man by the shoulders, then gently placed his hand on R' Gavriel's right cheek. "I don't believe it," he whispered. "This is amazing! We are family!"

"What?" R' Gavriel looked at Mr. Kleinman with disbelief. "I don't understand."

Mr. Kleinman turned away and called down the road towards his daughter and family. "Yocheved! Yocheved, come back here! Quickly!"

The Weinbergs turned around and hurried back to Mr. Kleinman and R' Gavriel. "What is it, Tatty? What's wrong?" Mrs. Weinberg asked anxiously.

Mr. Kleinman's eyes were glowing. "This man is our relative!" he exclaimed. "R' Gavriel, your great-grandfather was my grandmother's brother."

It took some time before they all had calmed down enough for Mr. Kleinman to explain. "R' Alexander came to America some time before the war," he told his spellbound audience. "As was customary at the time, he came on his own with the intention to earn enough money to support his family back home. With Hashem's help, he was very prosperous. When the war began, he sent for his own family and brought them to America. It didn't take him long to realize the danger that threatened every Jew remaining in Europe. Over the next two years, he brought seventeen other families to America, including ours. He found us apartments, bought us food and clothing, and set us up in various businesses." Mr. Kleinman paused. "We all owe him our lives."

Mrs. Weinberg's eyes were wet with emotion. "I can't believe it," she whispered. "When you came to us on Thursday night, I had this strange feeling that you were somehow related to us."

"That's right," Mr. Weinberg said, nodding his head. "You said so."

"But now we find out that it's true!"

R' Gavriel spent the remainder of *Shabbos* together with his new-found relatives, tracing the family history and enjoying many other topics of conversation. As he left the house together with the other men to *daven Maariv*, Mrs. Weinberg asked him to return to their home for *Havdalah*.

That *motzei Shabbos*, as R' Gavriel prepared to leave, the Weinbergs handed him another check. R' Gavriel was overwhelmed as he looked at the amount written on the check: ten thousand dollars.

"It's too much," he stammered. "I—I can't thank you enough!"

"On the contrary," Mrs. Weinberg said firmly. "It is we

who must thank you for allowing us in this small way to show gratitude to your great-grandfather for saving our family."

A BLESSING COME TRUE

Chazal say (Megillah 15a), "A blessing given by an ordinary person should not be considered insignificant." In the following story, this Chazal is brought to light.

Mr. and Mrs. Stern* were luckier than most: they had managed to survive the Holocaust, together with four of their eight children. America promised them a new chance, and the blessing of living in freedom. What they had not anticipated, however, was the hardship of supporting their family.

The Sterns were hard-pressed to make ends meet. Not only did they need to feed their family of six, but they also wanted to continue to provide their children with a Torah education. Fortunately, the children did what they could to help their parents out.

Bluma, one of the four children, was particularly concerned about the burden on her parents' shoulders. She wanted nothing more than to help her parents as much as she possibly could. Every chore and errand was considered a privilege in her eyes. Even outsiders marvelled at the respect and love she showed for her parents.

Names are fictitious.

When the time came for Bluma to marry, she was fortunate enough to find a life partner who was equally committed to a life of Torah and *mitzvos*. Bluma's extraordinary honor for her husband reflected the tremendous respect and concern she continued to have for her parents.

Bluma and her husband rented a spacious, five-room apartment. The day after their wedding, they asked Bluma's parents to move in with them. Thus, Bluma was able to continue to fulfill the *mitzvah* of *kibbud av v'aim* in its highest form.

Bluma's good deeds continued to grow as the years went past. There was only one thing that marred her happiness: she had not yet been blessed with a child.

Seventeen years had gone by. Bluma's mother had passed away long before, and her father was ninety-five years old. When he became ill, Bluma stayed faithfully at his side.

One morning, Bluma's father beckoned her closer. When she came near him, he handed her five large coins.

"These are *shekalim* coins," he told her. "They are used by parents to give to a *kohein* to redeem their first-born son. Bluma, with Hashem's help, you will give birth to a son and use these coins at his *pidyon haben*."

Bluma caressed her father's hands and thanked him for his blessing.

Shortly afterwards, Bluma's father was *niftar*. A year later, on *erev Yom Kippur*, Bluma gave birth to a baby boy. This son grew up to become a distinguished *posek* and leader in *klal Yisrael*.

FROSTBITE

"Throw your burden upon Hashem and He will provide for you." (Tehillim 55:23) At times, a person may be put in a situation where he clearly sees that Hashem is his only true provider. The following story related by Peretz Eichler clearly illustrates this point.

Peretz Eichler glanced at his watch one rainy spring night. It was 11:00 p.m.—the ideal time for a surprise inspection. Peretz was a part-time *mashgiach* for United Kosher supervision, and part of his job was supervising a bakery in a local supermarket. Though the bakery would be closed by now, the supermarket itself was still open, and he would be able to get inside to check on the ingredients used in the baking.

Peretz threw on his trenchcoat and drove through the drizzle to the supermarket. The parking lot was nearly empty; when he entered the store, he could see only one cashier and a couple of customers at the front of the supermarket.

Peretz made his way through the aisles to the bakery section. That area of the store was completely deserted. It was likely that no one would come back to that section until four o'clock in the morning, when the bakers arrived to begin work.

Peretz looked around at the supplies on the shelves, which appeared to be in order. Then he entered the walk-in freezer and started checking the supplies. It wasn't long before he started to feel the cold, despite the coat he was wearing. He wasted no time in checking the food on the shelves and then heading back to the door of the freezer.

Peretz pushed on the inside handle of the freezer door. Nothing happened. He frowned and pushed a little harder. Still nothing. He leaned back and jammed at the door with his shoulder. But it still didn't budge.

"What's going on here?" he grumbled in frustration. This time, instead of pushing the handle, he gave it a yank— and the handle came off in his hand.

Now Peretz panicked. He was stuck in the freezer with no way out, and no one was due to arrive for four more hours. It would be impossible for him to survive that long! He began banging on the door, all the while knowing that there was no one around to hear him. Then he noticed a small crack on the bottom of the door. He leaned down, took a deep breath of the fresh air, and began screaming for help.

Peretz had no idea how long he had been lying there, yelling for help. Had it been one minute? Five? Ten? Every second felt like a lifetime. He was taking another breath to call again when the freezer door suddenly opened.

Peretz stared upwards in shock. He quickly scrambled to his feet to face two young men, who were looking equally surprised.

"How did you get in here?" one of them exclaimed.

"I'm Rabbi Eichler from United Kosher supervision," Peretz hurriedly explained. "I went into the freezer to inspect the food, and somehow I got locked in. Thank you so much for coming to help me out! I would have frozen to death if not for you!

"Tell me, where are *you* coming from?"

"Actually, we're from Kentucky," one of the young men said. "We were just driving through New Jersey, and we stopped off to get something to chew on. We decided to get something from the bakery. When we got here, we saw the bakery was closed, but as we started to leave we heard some screaming coming from the freezer, so we opened the door."

"I can't thank you enough," Peretz said gratefully. "You literally saved my life."

"Do you know why you were saved?" the young man said to Peretz. "It says in Psalms, 'The one who trusts in G-d will be surrounded by kindness.'"

Peretz breathed a deep sigh. All he could manage to say was a whispered, "Baruch Hashem!"

JOURNEY TO HEALTH

Throughout their lives, people are affected by various influences. Sometimes, however, it is the pure influences from one's youth that can motivate his behavior at a specific time.

R' Mordche Lerner* was constantly on the move. After several years of generally neglecting of his health, he was completely worn out and exhausted. Reluctantly, he went to Mount Sinai hospital to be examined.

"You need a complete rest," the doctor declared. In addition to prescribing several medicines, he recommended that R' Mordche spend some time in Florida in an effort to regain his health. R' Mordche agreed to take a few weeks off his busy schedule and go to Miami.

R' Mordche soon found himself with a round-trip ticket to Fort Lauderdale in Florida. He found another *frum* couple

---
*Name is fictitious

travelling on the same plane and was grateful to accept their offer of a ride to Miami. He was sure that when the time came for his return flight, he would be able to find a way back to Fort Lauderdale in a similar fashion.

It was difficult for a man of R' Mordche's dynamism to do nothing but rest, but R' Mordche tried his best. He was disappointed to find that he was not getting any better, but two weeks had already passed and it was time to return to New York.

Two days before his scheduled flight, R' Mordche began to try to find a ride back to Fort Lauderdale. He attended *shul* as usual in the morning, and after *davening*, he began to ask several members of the *shul* if they knew of anyone going to Fort Lauderdale sometime in the next two days.

"Oh, you're going to see Doctor Strauss?" the first person said in reply.

"Well, actually," R' Mordche started to say, but the man continued. "Let me think... Hmmm. No, I'm sorry, I don't know anyone going. Maybe Mr. Levine would know." He pointed to a businessman who was busily folding his *tallis*.

"Dr. Strauss?" R' Mordche wondered to himself as he approached Mr. Levine. "Excuse me," he said aloud as the businessman looked up. "I'm looking for a ride to Fort Lauderdale, and I was told you might be able to help me."

"Going to Dr. Strauss, huh? Let's think." Mr. Levine rubbed at his nose as he considered the question. "Shaya Grossman might be going tomorrow morning. That's his brother over there. Why don't you ask him?"

More bewildered than ever, R' Mordche walked across the *shul* and tapped Shaya Grossman's brother on the shoulder. "Excuse me, but is your brother going to Fort Lauderdale tomorrow?"

The man turned around. "Shaya? Yes, that's right. He

has an appointment by Dr. Strauss. Is that where you're going? I'm sure he'll be glad to give you a ride."

This was too much for R' Mordche. "I'm sorry, but I've never even heard of Dr. Strauss until this morning. Exactly who is he?"

The man laughed. "He's an excellent doctor. Very popular, particularly with the *frum* community. He sees close to one hundred patients a day, and he's always booked for weeks ahead."

R' Mordche digested this information thoughtfully. To tell the truth, his enforced vacation in Miami had done him little good; he was still as exhausted and weak as he had been when he first arrived. If this Dr. Strauss was as good as everyone seemed to think, wouldn't it be worthwhile to try and see him?

The problem would be trying to get an appointment. Apparently, it took weeks to get to see him. R' Mordche was leaving the day after tomorrow. How could he possibly get to see the doctor before he left? Still, with his typical decisiveness, R' Mordche made up his mind to at least try to secure an appointment with Dr. Strauss. He still had one last day in Miami before he would go to Fort Lauderdale. Why not make an effort and see what happens?

Later that afternoon, one person told R' Mordche, "Mrs. Cohen might be able to help you. Here's her phone number. Good luck!"

R' Mordche dialed the number and waited a number of rings. Finally, a woman picked up the receiver. "Yes?"

"My name is Mordechai Lerner," R' Mordche began. "I was told you might be able to help me get an appointment to see—"

"Did you say your name is Mordechai Lerner?" Mrs. Cohen interrupted.

"Yes, I did."

"Rabbi Mordechai Lerner from Monsey?"

R' Mordche stared at the receiver. "Yes, I'm from Monsey," he said slowly. "Ah, do you know me?"

"I most certainly do!" Mrs. Cohen said warmly. "You helped my son get into *yeshivah* a few years ago."

R' Mordche cast his mind back and remembered. "Yes, of course," he said. "I'm sorry. I didn't realize you were the same Cohen. And how is Yanky doing these days?"

"*Baruch Hashem*, just wonderfully," Mrs. Cohen replied. "Now, Rabbi Lerner, what can I do for you?"

"I'm here in Florida for my health," R' Mordche explained.

"Oh, you're here to see Dr. Strauss?"

R' Mordche half-laughed. "Well, that's the point. I didn't even hear of Dr. Strauss until this morning, but I'd very much like to get an appointment to see him. Someone suggested you might be able to help me."

For a moment, Mrs. Cohen was silent. "It's very hard to get to see him," she said slowly. "He's very popular. It usually takes up to six weeks to get an appointment."

"I see." R' Mordche tried to keep the disappointment out of his voice. "Is there any way to get an appointment in less time? I'm supposed to return to Monsey in two days. I suppose I could postpone my flight for another week, but I really can't see myself staying for another month and a half."

"Well, let's see . . . Oh, of course! Why didn't I think of it before!" Mrs. Cohen's voice had suddenly strengthened. "Listen, Rabbi Lerner. I have an appointment myself to see Dr. Strauss tomorrow. Why don't you take it instead?"

"That's very kind of you, Mrs. Cohen, but I can't—"

"No, Rabbi Lerner, I insist. It's the least I can do for you after all the help you gave my son."

"Well, in that case," R' Mordche said slowly, "I will accept your kind offer. Thank you very much."

"Oh, you're welcome. The appointment is for ten-thirty." Mrs. Cohen thought for a moment. "Oh, and Rabbi Lerner, make sure that you tell them that your name is Cohen. The office doesn't allow people to transfer appointments. Don't tell them who you really are."

"Thank you," R' Mordche said again. "I really appreciate it."

The following morning, R' Mordche arrived at Dr. Strauss's medical office. The waiting room was filled with patients, many of whom were religious Jews. R' Mordche made his way through the well-appointed room and approached the secretary's window.

"Good morning, sir," the woman said pleasantly. "Do you have an appointment?"

"Yes," R' Mordche replied. "At ten-thirty."

"Your name, please?"

R' Mordche hesitated for a moment, then made up his mind. He didn't want to lie. "The appointment is for Cohen, but my name is Lerner," he said clearly. "I am taking Mrs. Cohen's appointment."

The secretary pressed her lips together and shook her head. "I'm sorry," she said with stiff politeness, "but we don't allow appointments to be transferred like that. I'm afraid you won't be able to see the doctor."

R' Mordche took a deep breath. "Could you just ask Dr. Strauss if he can see me? I'm leaving Florida tomorrow. This was the only way I could get to see the doctor before I left."

"I told you, sir, we don't allow—"

"Could you ask, though?"

"All right," the woman said reluctantly. "Wait here, please." She rose from her chair and disappeared through a door in the back of the room.

R' Mordche leaned against the wall and drummed his fingers on the counter. Had he done the right thing by admitting the truth about his name?

The secretary returned a minute later with a look of surprise on her face. "The doctor will see you," she told R' Mordche. "Please fill out this form and wait for me to call your name."

Delighted, R' Mordche wrote down all his medical information on the form and then sat down to await his turn. It was only a few minutes before he heard a nurse call his name. He stood and entered the doctor's office.

Dr. Strauss greeted him pleasantly and gave him a thorough examination. "Rabbi Lerner, you're in terrible condition," he said bluntly. "You ought to be hospitalized, but let's try something else first. I'm going to give you a treatment now, and I want you to come in again tomorrow."

"Tomorrow?" R' Mordche said, astonished. He would have thought that he would have to wait another few weeks before the doctor would agree to see him again.

"Yes, tomorrow. I'll squeeze you in somehow."

R' Mordche left the doctor's office feeling very impressed. Dr. Strauss was intelligent and capable. No wonder he was so popular! He quickly called the airline and arranged for a new reservation a week later. He hoped that Dr. Strauss would be able to see him more than once in this extra week of his stay.

A few days later, R' Mordche ran into his uncle, R' Lieberman.* "*Sholom Aleichem!*" R' Lieberman greeted him. "This is a nice surprise. I didn't know you'd come out to Florida, too. What brings you here, Mordche?"

**Name is fictitious*

R' Mordche explained the situation to his uncle. "Dr. Strauss gave me one more treatment," he finished. "I really think it helped. I wish there was some way I could get in to see him once or twice more before I have to go home."

R' Lieberman clapped his nephew on the shoulder. "Leave it to me," he said expansively. "I've been a patient with Dr. Strauss for over thirty years now. I've even got his home number. Let me talk to him and see if I can convince him to see you a few more times while you're here in Fort Lauderdale."

Sure enough, Dr. Strauss agreed to treat R' Mordche again. The day before his flight to New York, R' Mordche told Dr. Strauss, "I'll be returning to New York tomorrow, so I just want to say good-bye and thank you for taking the time and effort to help me like this."

Dr. Strauss smiled. "Why don't you come in again early tomorrow morning?" he suggested. "I can give you one last treatment before you go."

R' Mordche, delighted by this final opportunity, came to the doctor's office a few hours before his scheduled flight. After the last treatment, Dr. Strauss shook him warmly by the hand. "Good-bye, Mordche. Take good care of yourself."

R' Mordche was slightly startled to hear this *chassidic* pronunciation of his name coming so easily from the lips of a non-religious doctor. "Where did you pick up such an accent?" he asked curiously.

Dr. Strauss smiled and put his arm over R' Mordche's shoulders. "Believe it or not, I grew up in Williamsburg. I was inducted into the army during the war years, and I'm afraid that I was influenced by too many outside factors. That's why I'm like this today. But I still remember my childhood, and that's why I agreed to let you in on that first day when you didn't really have an appointment."

"What do you mean?" R' Mordche asked, fascinated.

"As soon as I heard your last name, I agreed to take you. I remember you and your family from Williamsburg. Your family always remained steadfast to the Torah, no matter what hardships you faced in life." Dr. Strauss lifted his arm and turned to face R' Mordche directly. "I wish you the best, Mordche," he said again. "My door is always open to you."

Bemused by this turn of events, R' Mordche hurried to the airport and made his flight in good time. On his return to Monsey, he arranged for a check-up by Mount Sinai hospital.

"I don't believe it!" the doctor exclaimed with astonishment as he completed his examination.

"What's wrong?" R' Mordche asked with anxiety.

"Nothing's wrong. That's the point." The doctor shook his head with disbelief. "Rabbi Lerner, I'm happy to tell you that you're in perfect health!"

"*Baruch Hashem,*" Rabbi Lerner said feelingly. "Hashem sent me the perfect *shaliach.*"

CARE FOR MY CHILDREN

At times, living in accordance with one's noblest instincts is a difficult task. There are those who nevertheless overcome this and display sublime character traits even amidst the most pressing situations.

August of 1970 had arrived, bringing with it the hot, humid days of summer. R' Yosef Schwab and his family were enjoying a well-deserved break in Highpoint State Park. The park, which is on the border of New York and Pennsylvania, is crossed by the Delaware River, making it a scenic spot for relaxation.

After spending some time hiking through the park, R' Yosef and his family arrived at the river, where they sat down to rest. R' Yosef was glancing around, enjoying the view, when he noticed a young man climb out of the river and onto a nearby boulder. As the man sat down to rest, he suddenly fell forward in a faint, hit his head on a rock and fell into the river.

R' Yosef and his wife ran into the river and they grabbed the man. Fighting against the current, they managed to drag the man out of the water and onto a surrounding embankment, where he began to administer artificial respiration.

R' Yosef's wife ran for help and brought back some firemen, who took over from R' Yosef. After a few minutes, the young man regained consciousness. He was muttering incoherently and was clearly in need of medical help.

The phone in the area was out of order, so Mrs. Schwab had to drive three miles to the ranger's office to call for an ambulance. Since they were in the park, however, he knew it would take some time for the ambulance to arrive. So the Schwab family continued to take care of the young man, covering him with blankets and trying to make him as comfortable as possible, until the ambulance arrived one hour later.

Even after the ambulance arrived, the Schwabs insisted on staying with the young man, until they were sure he was in good hands. And they continued to stay in touch with him until the young man's condition returned to normal.

A couple of months later, the Schwabs received a surprise visitor at their home in Elizabeth, NJ. The young man they had saved was standing, smiling, at their door.

"Hi, I'm Pat Mackentire. Remember me?"

He told the Schwabs that he was from Perth Amboy, N.J. where his father, a physician, had his own medical practice. He presented them with a bottle of whiskey and returned the blankets they had lent him.

"I can never thank you enough for what you did for me," he said sincerely. "You both saved my life!"

A few years after this incident, R' Yosef Schwab met Rabbi Edelstein, a new *mohel* who had just moved to Elizabeth from Perth Amboy.

"You say you're from Perth Amboy?" R' Yosef asked with interest. "Have you ever heard of a Dr. Mackentire?"

"Oh, sure. Everyone knows Dr. Mackentire! For years he's been treating all the *rabbeim*, and anyone who's affiliated with Torah, for free. He's shown a tremendous amount of kindness to the Torah community."

"Is that so?" R' Yosef said in amazement. "Let me tell you an interesting story!"

R' Yosef then went on to describe how he had saved Dr. Mackentire's son's life at Highpoint State Park, several years before. To the Schwab's the message was clear. Hashem had sent him and his wife to care for a child whose father cared for Hashem's children.

CATALYST FOR A CAR

Divine Providence is a real, potent factor in our lives. The challenge lies in taking a few moments to scrutinize events and "coincidences" and recognize them as Hashem's guiding Hand. The following story is told by Rabbi Eli Gewirtz.

R' Gewirtz squeezed out of his narrow seat in tourist class and went on a leg-stretching stroll to the back of the plane. The El Al flight was jammed with the usual conglomeration of varied tourists: black-hatted men with beards, teens in blue jeans with knapsacks, young couples flying back from a wedding, businessmen, families, hippies, and every other conceivable possibility.

As R' Gewirtz neared the back of the plane, he spotted an amiable-looking man dressed in western fashion, including polished cowboy boots and a fringed, embroidered shirt. All that was missing was the hat, and that was probably stored in the overhead luggage bin.

The man caught R' Gewirtz's gaze and smiled broadly. He held out his hand. "*Shalom,*" he said in a real southern drawl. "My name's Oscar."

"Eli Gewirtz," R' Gewirtz replied, shaking Oscar's hand.

"This is my first trip to Israel," Oscar confided. "As a Jew, I figured it's about time I visited our homeland."

R' Gewirtz commended Oscar on his deep Jewish feelings and spent over an hour with him in pleasant conversation. By the end of the flight, the two men had exchanged addresses and promised to keep in touch.

When R' Gewirtz returned home from Eretz Yisrael and recovered from his jet lag, he sat down and penned a letter to Oscar. The chance encounter on the plane might yet lead to the awakening of the latent spark of Oscar's *yiddishe neshamah*. At first, Oscar was a faithful correspondent who wrote back often, but with time, the letters became fewer and fewer until they stopped completely.

One morning, as Mrs. Gewirtz served breakfast to her husband, she remarked, "You know, the car is really on its last legs. It took me ages to get it started yesterday."

"Maybe I can have it looked at," R' Gewirtz suggested as he drank his coffee.

Mrs. Gewirtz shook her head. "We've spent so much money on it lately. Let's face it. It's an old car, and we've squeezed every drop of use out of it already. I know it won't be easy, but I really think we ought to buy a new one."

R' Gewirtz grimaced. "I wouldn't mind a new car, either, but where are we going to find the money for one?" He sighed and shook his head. "We'll just have to manage with our old 'clunker,' that's all."

It was already late. R' Gewirtz finished eating hurriedly, *bentched*, thanked his wife, and went outside to start the car. He'd have to drive fast to get to *kollel* on time.

Unfortunately, the car had other plans. When R' Gewirtz turned the key in the ignition, the engine sputtered and died. He tried again. The engine wouldn't even turn over.

R' Gewirtz sat there for a long moment, staring at the driving wheel. What was he going to do now?

Sitting there wouldn't help. He scrambled out of the car and stood at the curb, scanning the passing cars in the faint hope of seeing a familiar face. Maybe a friend would pass by, someone who could help him start the car.

Less than five minutes had passed before a car turned the corner and approached. R' Gewirtz, squinting into the distance, saw a bearded face behind the wheel that looked familiar. Assuming it was one of the members of the *kollel*, he waved frantically. Even if he couldn't get the car started, at least he could get to *kollel*!

The car slowed and approached. R' Gewirtz's smile of relief changed to a puzzled frown as the car pulled to the side of the road. He didn't know the man behind the wheel at all.

The man rolled down his car window and leaned out. "Hey, there," he drawled. "Do you know a Rabbi Gewirtz?"

R' Gewirtz blinked. "I'm Rabbi Gewirtz," he said automatically.

The car door flew open and the man leaped out. He was wearing cowboy boots, white trousers, and a screen-printed shirt. A cowboy hat was in prominent view on the passenger front seat. "Rabbi!" he beamed, covering a startled R' Gewirtz with hugs and kisses. "Do you remember me? I'm Oscar!"

"Oscar," R' Gewirtz gasped. "I didn't recognize you with your beard." Then, recovering himself, he took a step back and managed a more normal welcome. "It's wonderful to see you, Oscar. What brings you to these parts?"

Oscar slapped R' Gewirtz familiarly on the back. "Well, after that trip I took to Israel, I decided that I belonged there. All Jews do. So I settled all my business affairs, and I'm moving to Israel next week. Now, I'm driving around the country to say good-bye to all my family and friends." He beamed again. "You're my last stop, Rabbi Gewirtz. I've come to say good-bye to you."

R' Gewirtz, touched that Oscar considered him a good friend after corresponding with him a few times, invited him to come into the house. Mrs. Gewirtz responded to her oddly-dressed visitor with aplomb and served the two men coffee and cake. They lingered over their refreshments, chatting.

"So where will you stay until your flight next week?" R' Gewirtz asked.

Oscar shrugged. "In a hotel, I suppose."

"Absolutely not," R' Gewirtz said firmly. "You can stay here." It was his last chance to show Oscar a little more about

Yiddishkeit. He wasn't about to let this final chance slip away.

Oscar accepted the invitation with pleasure, and R' Gewirtz took full advantage of the extra time to discuss Torah and *Yiddishkeit* with his Western visitor. Oscar enjoyed his stay immensely, but all too soon it was time for him to leave.

The night before Oscar's flight to Eretz Yisrael, he said at the supper table, "You know, since I'm flying to Israel and settling there, I don't need my car anymore. I don't suppose you know anyone who could use a car?"

R' Gewirtz could feel the heat of his wife's gaze. He didn't dare look at her. The silence grew strained.

Oscar didn't seem to notice. "You mean there's nobody you know who needs a car?"

R' Gewirtz felt his face redden. "Well, to be honest," he said finally, "our car is very old. In fact, it's dying." He stopped short. He couldn't bring himself to continue.

Oscar chuckled and gave R' Gewirtz yet another friendly clout on the back. "Rabbi Gewirtz, say no more. The car is yours!"

A chance encounter on a plane and a desire to help bring another Jew back to *Yiddishkeit.* Who would have dreamed it would bring the Gewirtzes a badly-needed car?

LOST AND FOUND

R' Yosef Lieberman looked up at the ceiling of his three-family home and sighed. The spreading corrosion and the plaster on the floor was a clear indication that he would be in for some tedious work. No doubt there was a leak somewhere that was causing the problem.

R' Lieberman got up on his ladder and began carefully peeling off the rest of the plaster. After some time, he was able to break through the ceiling. He pushed the rubble to the side to clear some space so he could get a good look at what was going on.

"Aha!" he grunted after a few more minutes.

The hole in the ceiling was directly beneath the radiator in the apartment above. And the radiator was leaking.

He continued to methodically clean away the rubble as he worked. Suddenly, a glitter caught his eye. He reached into the hole in the ceiling, and discovered to his amazement that he was holding a beautiful diamond ring.

R' Lieberman surmised that the ring must have fallen through the crack surrounding the radiator pipe in the apartment above. Clearly, a tenant had dropped the ring and had been unable to find it. But R' Lieberman had been renting out these apartments for over twenty years. That meant that the only way to find out who the ring belonged to was to contact each of those people.

The task was a daunting one. But R' Lieberman was undeterred. And so, armed with a copy of the Brooklyn telephone book, R' Lieberman began calling his past tenants to ask if they knew anything about a missing ring.

"No, I didn't lose a ring."

"Nope, not me."

"I'm afraid not. Thanks for calling anyway."

And so it went. No one he spoke to had any knowledge of a missing ring. Still, R' Lieberman continued making his calls, moving back to earlier tenants, until he finally called a family who had lived there quite some time before.

"Did you ever lose a ring when you were living in my

apartment?" he asked the woman who answered the phone.

"Why, yes, as a matter of fact I did. Why do you ask?"

"I found a ring beneath the floor of the apartment."

"Really?" she asked in excitement. "I lost my engagement ring when I was living there. That was nineteen years ago, right after I was married. My husband and I got down on our hands and knees and searched all over, but we just couldn't find it. You found it beneath the floor? It must have slipped through a crack. No wonder we couldn't find it."

"Well, I have it now," R' Lieberman reassured her.

"That's wonderful! Thank you so much!"

R' Lieberman put down the phone and smiled. The satisfaction of fulfilling a *mitzvah* and bringing happiness to this family was worth more to him than all the money in the world.

SAVED BY THE ENEMY

Shlomo Hamelech states, "There is a time for everything under the heavens: a time to be born, a time to die..." (Koheles 3:1,2) The following story is told by a Holocaust survivor.

Moshe* trudged through the deep snow, shivering in his rags and shuffling along as quickly as he could to avoid yet another beating from the overseer. He and the other concentration camp inmates had already been savagely beaten earlier that morning before they were ordered out of the

---
**Name is fictitious.*

camp. Now, he marched along as best as he could, one of a double line of men who were ordered to build railroad tracks for their enemies.

Soon, they arrived at the unfinished tracks. Moshe wearily bent over his task, hammering and banging all day long as they laid new rails. The overseer watched his prisoners carefully, eager to spot the first sign of slacking or laziness that would allow him to unleash a fresh string of expletives and another beating.

Whenever the inmates completed a section of the track, a train was sent down the mountainside to test the efficiency of the newly-finished rails. Moshe and the others quaked at the thought of their tormentors finding fault in their work.

There came a time when Moshe felt that all his strength was gone. His arms trembled as he tried to lift up the heavy hammer. Feebly, he pounded at the track as the rails swam in front of his eyes.

Suddenly, a shout rang out. "Everyone off the tracks! They're sending a train down!" All the inmates ran off the tracks to safety—except Moshe. Utterly exhausted, he simply collapsed right where he was, lying across the tracks as the train thundered down the mountainside.

Later, he found out how his life had been saved. The overseer had spotted Moshe lying on the track and pounced on him. "Lazy, dirty Jew!" the man bellowed. "Get up and get back to work!" When Moshe did not respond, the overseer exploded with rage and reached out a beefy hand to grab the unconscious Jew by his ragged shirt and lift him bodily off the tracks.

"How dare you disobey me?" he bellowed, shaking Moshe violently before tossing him to one side with disgust. Moments later, the train roared along the tracks, shaking the rails from side to side as it passed over the point where

Moshe had been lying only a minute or two before.

Years later, when Moshe had emigrated to America, he related this story to R' Aharon Kotler. Reb Aharon smiled and noted, "If it is Hashem's will that one should live, then even a murderer can be the savior."

A MOTHER'S KERCHIEF

> *Observing mitzvos changes a person; their spirituality affects one's very being. The more devotion one invests in a mitzvah, the more intensely it will affect him. The following story, told by a kollel member of Beth Medrash Govoha of Lakewood, is a case in point.*

Naftali Leibowitz* was only nineteen years old when his mother was diagnosed as having a terminal illness. At such a young age, the prospect of death could be devastating. Naftali derived what comfort he could from his mother's strength and tenacity.

Mrs. Leibowitz was a truly remarkable woman. She refused to accept other people's pity. On the contrary, she was determined to help others in similar situations. She would visit terminally ill patients, offering comfort and support for their emotional and physical pain.

If anyone would try to do the same for her, she brushed such sympathy aside. Her condition slowly grew worse and her pain was often excruciating, but her children never

---
* *Name is fictitious.*

heard her complain about anyone or anything. Naftali only heard her cry out once from the pain, and she immediately began to apologize afterward for making her family feel uncomfortable.

Mrs. Leibowitz's illness progressed inexorably. She was hospitalized and given constant care as the medical staff tried to ease her pain and discomfort. Some time later, she fell into a coma, lying white and still in her hospital bed without responding to anything around her.

It was more than Naftali could bear. He hated to see his mother, the fiery power house of *shemiras hamitzvos* and *yiras shamayim*, in such a helpless condition. He visited her silent hospital room daily, desperately searching her face for some response, some improvement in her condition. His mother couldn't leave him like this! He needed her *chizuk*, her encouragement. If only she would somehow recover!

But the coma persisted. Nothing changed.

One day, as Naftali prepared to leave for the hospital, a sudden impulse prompted him to bring the new *tichel* he had purchased for his mother along to the hospital. He had bought the new kerchief just before Mrs. Leibowitz lapsed into her coma, as a small token to show her how much he cared for her and how much he appreciated her as a living example of *Yiddishkeit*. Perhaps, he thought, it would make him feel better to see his beloved mother wearing the *tichel* he had bought for her.

Soon after he entered the quiet hospital room and sat down, a nurse came in to check on Mrs. Leibowitz's condition. Naftali took the *tichel* out of his jacket pocket and explained.

"I'll be glad to put it on for you," the nurse said soothingly. "Let me just take off the old one . . ."

The nurse gingerly lifted Mrs. Leibowitz's head and

removed the older kerchief she was wearing. Naftali clearly saw his mother jerk and her facial muscles tighten -- the first response he'd seen at all since she lapsed into her coma.

Then the nurse placed the new kerchief on Mrs. Leibowitz's head. "There," she said, tying it firmly into place. As she did so, Mrs. Leibowitz's face relaxed. Her eyelids fluttered, and she even seemed to smile.

Naftali blinked back tears and gave a smile of his own. Even in her comatose state, his mother had taught him a lesson. She had always been so meticulous with the laws of modesty throughout her life that her body had been trained to react to immodesty. When her hair had been uncovered, even for just a moment, she had reacted with distress. Now, with the *tichel* safely back in place, she had relaxed and almost smiled with approval.

Mrs. Leibowitz was *niftar* shortly thereafter, but the last lesson she had given to her son would remain with Naftali for the rest of his life.

3
FEELINGS AND CONCERNS

Flight from Heaven

Strictly Business

A Healing Visit

Lest Others Stumble

Concern for Klal Yisrael

Heavenly Reliance

A Moment of Truth

Long-Term Success

Designated Livelihood

Admonishment with Love

Sagacious Rebuke

3
Feelings and Concerns

FLIGHT FROM HEAVEN

The following story was related by Rav Moshe Aaron Stern, mashgiach of Yeshivas Kaminetz, who heard it directly from the great tzaddik Rav Aryeh Levin.

Reb Yosef was the driving force behind the financial committee of the Bikur Cholim Hospital in Yerushalayim. With the financial burden of the hospital on his shoulders, he had enough work to keep him occupied all day and half the night. Somehow, though, Reb Yosef found the time to take an active role in the day-to-day management of the hospital. And wherever he went, he took a few moments to talk to the patients, cheer them up and make them feel that someone cared about them.

Despite his advanced age, Reb Yosef did not slow down in his dedication to the hospital and its patients. But time and age eventually caught up to him. When he was seventy-five years old, his deteriorating health forced him to become hospitalized. His situation worsened rapidly, and in a matter of days, he was lying motionless in his bed, barely conscious.

One day, Reb Yosef had a distinguished visitor. The well-known *tzaddik*, Rav Aryeh Levin, came to his room and sat down near Reb Yosef's bed. Reb Yosef barely acknowledged his visitor; he lay there, his eyes unmoving, his breathing shallow.

R' Aryeh sat silently by the bed of his friend, watching his face with compassion. Suddenly, R' Aryeh jumped up in alarm. Reb Yosef had lost consciousness! R' Aryeh immediately summoned the doctors, who flew into the room and began shouting orders to each other.

R' Aryeh retreated into the hall, where he stood saying *Tehillim*. The minutes dragged by, turning into hours, and still the doctors were inside Reb Yosef's room. Finally, after two hours had passed, one of the doctors emerged from the room.

"What is happening?" R' Aryeh inquired.

The doctor turned to him, an expression of wonder on his face. "He's all right!" he exclaimed. "It's unbelievable, but the patient has regained consciousness. I was sure that we were going to lose him."

The rest of the doctors made their way out of the room, more than one of them shaking his head in disbelief.

The senior doctor stopped for a moment by R' Aryeh. "You can go back in now," he told him.

R' Aryeh stepped back into the room. He walked quietly over to the bed, where R' Yosef was now resting calmly.

"How are you feeling, R' Yosef?" R' Aryeh asked softly.

Reb Yosef's eyes lit up. "Oh, thank you for staying here!

I have something wondrous to tell you.

"When I lost consciousness, I was taken up to *shomayim*, to the Heavenly Court. I came before the judges, who are the *tzaddikim* of the past generation. They asked me if I had kept Torah and *mitzvos*.

"'Yes, I did,' I replied.

"The moment I said those words, all the angels that had been created by my *mitzvos* and Torah learning were asked to step forward. Armies of angels dressed in white came before the court, each one testifying to a *mitzvah* that I did.

"When all the angels had come forward, the court asked, 'Have you done any *aveiros*?'

"I was unable to answer, but I put my head down in shame. The court declared, 'All prosecuting angels that were created by this man's sins should come forward.'

"A great fear came upon me, and I watched as armies of prosecuting angels came forward.

"The court had begun tabulating the results, when suddenly another *tzaddik* entered the courtroom. All the judges stood up in respect.

"'Why have you come here?' they asked him.

"'I heard that you were judging Reb Yosef, so I came personally to testify. I was one of the head rabbinical leaders of the Bikur Cholim hospital before leaving the world. I testify that Reb Yosef did his job with absolute dedication. His handling of the money of this institution was executed in the most honest and trustworthy manner possible. His *ehrlichkeit* was a great *kiddush Hashem*.'

"As soon as the *tzaddik* finished speaking, he walked out of the room. The other *tzaddikim* on the *beis din* discussed the matter among themselves. Eventually they decided that they would allow me to return to the world, so I could correct and repent all my sins.

"I left the courtroom and began walking. I was all alone. Mountains and valleys stretched out before me, and I had no idea which way to go to get back to this world.

"As I came over a hill, I noticed a man coming toward me. He called out, 'Reb Yosef! Do you remember me?'

"'No, I don't,' I said.

"'You may not remember me. But I remember you!

"'You come from a small *shtetl* in Lithuania. The custom in your *shul* was that on Friday night after *davening*, all the poor people would line up in the back by the door, and each man leaving would invite one person home to share a *Shabbos* meal with him.

"'I, too, joined the line. However, because of my huge physique and my personal appearance, no one was willing to take me home.

"'You, Reb Yosef, were a little boy then. You and your father were ready to leave *shul*. Your father sized me up, then told you to come home, and I was left there alone.

"'After several minutes, you returned and told me that you had convinced your father to invite me, by telling him, "If that poor person has nothing to eat for *Shabbos*, then I, too, will not eat this *Shabbos*." And so I came to eat the *Shabbos* meal in your home.

"'Your *chesed* was more than a simple gesture. I had come to your city with nothing to eat for *Shabbos*. You literally saved my life.

"'Now that I have met you again, tell me: Is there anything I can do for you?'

"'Actually, there is!' I related to him all that had transpired. 'Now I am looking for the way back to the earthly world. Can you tell me where to go?'

"The man told me exactly how to get back: around this mountain, over that hill, through another valley. And as you can see, R' Aryeh, I found my way back."

Reb Yosef knew that his time on this earth was limited. He immediately began doing *teshuvah* and performing as many *mitzvos* as he could. Exactly thirty days later, Reb Yosef passed away—without doubt, having done complete *teshuvah*.

STRICTLY BUSINESS

The Torah commands each one of us to seek peace and love our fellow Jew. In practice, there are many obstacles in the way of our attaining these middos. Nevertheless, it is incumbent upon the Torah Jew to overcome these tests.

One situation where ill feelings can be created is at a din Torah (court case). Two people who are at odds with each other are most likely to harbor feelings of resentment.

The following story, related by R' Chaim Leib Weinstein of Yerushalayim, illustrates how a din Torah can sometimes take on a completely different appearance.

In 1949, food was very hard to come by in Eretz Yisrael. Many of the people living there had a difficult time eking out a livelihood and supporting their families.

Nassan Eliezer Grossman was among those struggling to make ends meet. He made his meager living selling milk from door to door in the streets of Yerushalayim. The job was hard, and the pay was small, but eventually R' Nassan managed to carve out a niche for himself. After several years, he acquired a number of steady customers, who appreciated his hard work and honesty.

But then R' Nassan became ill. The doctors declared that he would have to be hospitalized for several weeks. And so R' Nassan had to leave his job and enter the hospital, where thoughts of his suffering family continued to plague him. "What will they live on when I am not there to provide for them?" he wondered. R' Nassan tried to strengthen his faith and ease the burden on his mind, while he concentrated on getting better.

He had no way of knowing that his troubles were only beginning.

Several days after R' Nassan entered the hospital, word came to him that another man, Pinchas Ravitz, had taken over his milk route.

"It only makes sense," R' Nassan thought. "After all, my customers do need milk while I'm in the hospital. Someone's got to do it."

Still, no matter how reasonable it sounded, the thought of not having his business to come back to when he finally left the hospital was a daunting one. But R' Nassan swallowed his painful questions and placed his trust in Hashem. One way or another, he knew, Hashem would provide for him.

After several weeks, R' Nassan was finally able to leave the hospital. That first evening, he started to consider the different options that were open to him in rebuilding his livelihood. His thoughts were interrupted by a knock on the door.

R' Nassan opened the door. "Can I help you?" he inquired of the stranger standing outside.

"My name is Pinchas Ravitz," the man introduced himself.

R' Nassan immediately recognized the name. "What can I do for you?" he asked gently.

R' Pinchas placed his hand in his pocket and drew out a handful of coins. "I came to bring you your money."

"Money?" R' Nassan asked, confused. "Money for what?"

"You see," R' Pinchas explained, "when I heard that you were hospitalized, I realized that you would not be able to sell your milk, and I know that this is your only source of income. So I took it upon myself to sell the milk for you during your absence.

"Here is the money I received. It's all yours."

R' Nassan couldn't believe what he was hearing. "I can't take the money from you! After all, you did all the work. The money belongs to you."

"Oh, no," R' Pinchas insisted. "The money is yours!"

Neither man would give in to the other. And so they went to a *din Torah*—to discover who would be required to keep the money that neither one wanted for himself.

A HEALING VISIT

Our Torah leaders utilize their every moment for learning and practicing the Torah. Nevertheless, it is these very same leaders who always seem to find the time to care for and share in the troubles of others.

As a young boy, R' Yitzchak Brandwein lived in Williamsburg with his family. When he was eight years old, little Yitzchak was taken ill and brought to Beth Israel Hospital on the East Side. The doctors assured his parents that the boy would recover, but it would be necessary for him to remain in the hospital for several days for observation and treatment.

"Don't worry, he'll be all right," the doctor said heartily. "We'll just keep him here for a couple of days to make sure there's no relapse. You can take him home on Sunday night."

Sunday night! The Brandweins stared at the doctor. That meant that Yitzchak would have to remain in the hospital over *Shabbos*!

There was nothing they could do about it, so they resolved to spend *Shabbos* in the hospital together with their eight-year-old son. Hospitalization was traumatic enough for a child of his age without having to spend *Shabbos* alone in such circumstances. Unfortunately, events proved otherwise and the Brandweins were unable to remain in the hospital. Reluctantly, they took their leave of little Yitzchak late on Friday afternoon, promising to return as soon as possible on *Motzei Shabbos*.

"We'll be thinking about you the entire *Shabbos*," his father said encouragingly. "We'll leave your *siddur* right here for you so you can *daven*."

"And here is some cake *l'kovod Shabbos*," his mother added, forcing herself to smile at the hapless little boy in the hospital bed. "It will help you have some *oneg Shabbos*."

Yitzchak smiled bravely back. He hated the idea of spending *Shabbos* in the hospital, and being alone would make it even worse. Still, he was determined to make the best of it. He'd manage somehow!

Shabbos proved to be long and lonely. Yitzchak *davened* the *tefillos* and ate the *seudos* and the cake his mother had left behind, but he felt hollow inside. Where was the holy, joyous atmosphere he always felt at home? The hospital seemed too sterile, too impersonal, for *Shabbos*. As the long afternoon dragged on, he laid back in bed and stared at the ceiling, wishing there was some way the time could pass more quickly. He couldn't wait to see his family again and finally be able to go home.

Just then, a soft knock sounded on the door to his room. Yitzchak sat up in surprise as the door opened. Who could it be? The nurses didn't bother to knock before they came inside. Could he possibly have a visitor?

To his astonishment, he did indeed have a visitor that *Shabbos* afternoon. It was no ordinary visitor, either. Yitzchak could hardly believe his eyes as Rav Avraham Yehoshua Heschel, the Kopicznitzer Rebbe (1887-1963), entered the room with a gentle smile.

The Rebbe was acquainted with the Brandweins and had heard about Yitzchak's situation. Knowing how Yitzchak must feel to be all alone over *Shabbos*, he had walked over two miles in the hot sun, just to visit the young boy in the hospital.

"Good *Shabbos*, Yitzchak," the Rebbe said as he sat down in a chair near Yitzchak's bed. "How are you feeling today?"

"*Baruch Hashem*, much better," Yitzchak stammered, flushing. He still found it hard to believe that the Rebbe had come all the way to Beth Israel Hospital to visit *him!*

The conversation continued with awkward pauses. After all, an age gap of such proportions is difficult to bridge, particularly since Yitzchak was very much in awe of his visitor. The Rebbe, undeterred, continued to chat with the boy, smiling encouragingly and listening with authentic interest to his answers.

After several minutes, the Rebbe noticed a set of Chinese checkers lying on the little table next to Yitzchak's bed. "Are these yours?" he asked, holding up the board.

"Uh, yes, they are," Yitzchak replied.

"Well, then," the Rebbe smiled, "why don't you explain

the rules to me, and we'll play a game or two?"

The Rebbe sat with the eight-year-old boy and played Chinese checkers with him. Finally, after over an hour, the Rebbe stood.

"I'm afraid I must be going now," he said apologetically. "But I must thank you for a most interesting afternoon."

The Rebbe smiled and blessed him, then walked out of the room to begin his two-mile hike back to his *beis midrash* on Henry Street, where he would spend what was left of the afternoon immersed in Torah.

Silence returned to Yitzchak's hospital room, but he no longer felt depressed and lonely. He knew he would always cherish the memory of the *tzaddik's* smile and the caring that had brought the Rebbe to the hospital to visit a sick boy and brighten up his *Shabbos*.

LEST OTHERS STUMBLE

Love and concern for others are indeed noble attributes. However, a true ohev Yisrael is concerned with his fellow Jew's spiritual behavior as well.

R' Chanina Hertzberg considered it a great privilege to be a *talmid* of his esteemed *rebbe*, Rav Shlomo Freifeld, the late *rosh yeshivah* of Yeshivas Shaarei Yoshuv. The subsequent closeness allowed R' Chanina to witness Rav Freifeld's unique *Ahavas Yisrael*, his great love and concern for his fellow Jew.

One summer, R' Chanina drove Rav Freifeld from the *yeshivah's* bungalow colony to Woodridge. He parked the car outside the bakery and went inside to purchase coffee and cake for the *rosh yeshivah*. Upon his return, he found Rav Freifeld looking troubled as he stared out the car window.

"What is it, *rebbe*?" R' Chanina asked anxiously. He followed Rav Freifeld's gaze. A few young boys were standing in front of a pharmacy, waiting to catch a bus. R' Chanina could not discern the problem until he looked past the boys at the pharmacy window, where several indecent magazines were on prominent display. Then R' Chanina understood: Rav Freifeld was upset that the magazines were displayed so openly. Anyone who waited at that bus stop could not help but see them.

"Please do me a favor, R' Chanina," Rav Freifeld requested. "Go ask the owner of the store how much profit he expects to make from the sales of the magazines that are displayed in the store window."

R' Chanina nodded and hurried off to the pharmacy, which was then owned by a non-religious Jew. He approached the owner and said courteously, "Excuse me, but there is a very great rabbi outside and he has asked me to find out how much profit you will make this summer from the sale of the magazines in your display window."

The owner looked at R' Chanina, astonished. "What? What are you talking about? I never heard such a crazy question in my life! What does a great rabbi want to know about my magazines, anyway?"

Patiently, R' Chanina explained. "The rabbi is very disturbed that people who innocently walk past your window are exposed to indecent magazines. He would like to know how much profit you make on selling these magazines over the summer."

"Well, I—" The man stopped. "I don't—" He stopped again. "All right," he said finally. "If that's what the rabbi wants to know, I'll try and figure it out." He sat down behind the cash register and scribbled on a scrap of paper for a few minutes. Then he looked up. "Tell the rabbi that I'll probably make about one hundred and fifty dollars profit on those magazines over the summer. Just tell me one thing. Why does he have to know?"

R' Chanina, who didn't know the answer to that question himself, merely smiled. "Thank you," he said politely before retreating into the sunshine and making his way back to the car. He opened the door, sat down, and reported. "*Rebbe,* the man says he makes about one hundred and fifty dollars profit on the magazines."

Rav Freifeld nodded and reached into his jacket for his checkbook. He took out a pen and wrote a check for $150.00. He handed the check to R' Chanina and said, "Please go back into the pharmacy and give the owner this check. Ask him if he will at least consider taking the magazines out of the front window, so that people passing by do not have to see them."

R' Chanina took the check from the *rosh yeshivah* and hurried back to the pharmacy. By this time, the owner was standing in the doorway, his face clearly expressing his bafflement.

R' Chanina handed over the check and repeated Rav Freifeld's request. The man looked at the check for a long minute, then slowly raised his head and stared across the street at the car where Rav Freifeld was patiently waiting.

Shaking his head, the man handed the check back to R' Chanina. "Give the rabbi back his check," he said. "He doesn't have to give me the money. If it bothers the rabbi so much, I'll take them out of the window and put them on a display in a less public place. I understand what the rabbi is trying to tell me. Don't worry. I'll take care of it right away."

R' Chanina thanked the man and went back to the car,

happy to report success to Rav Freifeld. As he started the motor and drove away, R' Chanina could not help but marvel at his *rebbe's* deep concern for others and his success in protecting his fellow Jews from an inadvertent transgression.

Concern for Klal Yisrael

Torah leaders shoulder the responsibility and care for all of klal Yisrael. The following story related by a talmid of Rav Aharon Kotler is a case in point.

Hagaon Reb Aharon Kotler established the *yeshivah* of *Beis Medrash Govoha* in Lakewood in the years after World War II. Those that were privileged to come to the *yeshivah* during his lifetime were awed by his fiery erudition, vast knowledge in Torah and his *yiras shamayim*. But there was another side to Reb Aharon, as well: he felt a fatherly responsibility for all of *klal Yisrael* and possessed a great love for each and every fellow Jew. His selfless dedication to countless *chesed* projects, both in America and Eretz Yisrael, serves as ample proof of this, but he also reached out to the individual with sensitivity and caring.

Many Jews who met Reb Aharon would pour out their hearts and beg him for advice or assistance. There was one *chassidic* man, however, who often approached Reb Aharon with a different purpose in mind. He would verbally attack the *rosh yeshivah*, angrily voicing his negative opinions of everything Reb Aharon ever did. His vitriolic comments were often illogical and opinionated, but he never hesitated to voice them.

Reb Aharon listened to the man's diatribes in silence. He knew that this *yid* had suffered terribly in the Holocaust and had lost his entire family. The *yid's* angry, loud-voiced opinions were nothing more than manifest evidence of the terrible scars on his personality. If it made the man feel better to complain, Reb Aharon was willing to listen.

One *yeshivah bachur* who lived in the same neighborhood as him had often witnessed the encounters between the Holocaust survivor and his *rebbe*. He knew the *chassid* very well and was hardly surprised to see the man acting with such rudeness and bitterness towards Reb Aharon. The *bachur* was impressed by the *rosh yeshivah*'s patience, but the true extent of Reb Aharon's tremendous concern for this particular *yid* only came to light a few weeks after Reb Aharon's *petirah*.

The man began to ask for assistance from the local community charity. Many people were puzzled by this sudden turn of events. This man had never needed help in the past. If the *yid* needed financial support, why hadn't he asked for it until now?

Slowly, the truth came out: Reb Aharon had been discreetly supporting the *chassid* over the years. Despite the man's constant complaints and accusations, Reb Aharon overlooked his angry bitterness and saw only a fellow Jew who needed help. Not only had he patiently listened to the man for years, he had given him a steady stipend to alleviate his poverty. To a *gadol* of his stature, a fellow Jew in need deserved all the help he could offer.

HEAVENLY RELIANCE

Praiseworthy is the man who is able to live his daily life with the complete faith that Hashem is with him in all that he does.

Hagaon Harav Eliyahu Henkin (1880-1973), the great Torah leader and *posek*, was always careful to put the well-being of others above his own concerns.

A case in point was his desire to be buried in America, instead of having his *aron* taken to Eretz Yisrael. He explained that if he were brought to Eretz Yisrael for burial, other people will want to follow suit, and this might bring financial hardship upon families who really could not afford this expense.

But while Rav Henkin felt this way himself, he certainly did not insist on this for others. When his Rebbetzin was *niftar*, Rav Henkin made arrangements for her *aron* to be brought to Eretz Yisrael.

R' Moshe Margulin, who was close to Rav Henkin, had heard that Rav Henkin would not be escorting the *aron* to Eretz Yisrael. He approached Rav Henkin and asked, "Who will be making the arrangements for the burial in Eretz Yisrael?"

"My close friend, Rav Aryeh Levin, will probably take care of it," Rav Henkin replied.

"Does R' Aryeh know about it? Should we contact R' Aryeh to make sure that he knows what to do?" R' Moshe persisted.

"Oh, that won't be necessary," Rav Henkin reassured him. "I'm sure he'll find out about it."

In time, the *aron* did go to Eretz Yisrael, and the arrangements were made. But R' Margulin did not hear any details about how this had come about until he met R' Aryeh himself, some time later.

"I've been wondering about the arrangements that were made for Rebbetzin Henkin's funeral," he said to R' Aryeh. "Do you happen to know anything about it?"

"Actually, the whole thing was very interesting," said R' Aryeh. "I had been unaware of the death of the Rebbetzin. One morning, as I was walking outside, I noticed that the *chevra kadisha* was attending a funeral. I came over, and I asked the *chevra kadisha* who the *niftar* was. They told me that it was a lady named Henkin from America.

"Of course, I immediately recognized the name, and I made arrangements for the rest of the funeral."

Only then did R' Margulin become aware of the great *bitachon* that Rav Henkin possessed. And indeed, Rav Henkin had proved right: R' Aryeh *would* be there, one way or another.

A MOMENT OF TRUTH

The routine of everyday living can leave us with little time for thinking of others. Sometimes, however, a single moment's thought can be acted upon and cause one to reach great heights.

R' David* sighed as he walked off the plane in Harristown*, a small, southern city. He'd often come here on fundraising

---
* All names and places are fictitious.

trips; oil was a big business here in Harristown, and he'd always hoped that he would be able to convince the affluent Jews of the city to contribute generously to his cause. Somehow, though, the people of Harristown were all extremely reluctant to give *tzedakah*. Nevertheless, year after year, R' Kahan made the effort to return to Harristown and try to collect a little bit more than the year before.

R' Kahan spent the next several days making his usual rounds of wealthy Jewish businessmen. Each one gave willingly enough, but it was a paltry amount in comparison with the sums that R' Kahan knew these men could afford.

After close to a week in Harristown, R' Kahan found himself studying a certain name on his list: Sam Hendon. Hendon, the president of an oil corporation and a very wealthy man, was always too busy to talk to R' Kahan. In all the years that R' Kahan had been coming to Harristown, he had never actually been able to make contact with the wealthy industrialist. There was little reason to think that things would be different this time, but R' Kahan's optimism asserted itself and he placed the call.

Much to his surprise, the secretary acted almost human. Instead of her usual chilly "I'm sorry, but Mr. Hendon is in conference. You'll have to try again," the secretary merely said, "One moment, please," and put R' Kahan through to her boss.

"Hello, Rabbi," boomed a Texas drawl over the line. "What can I do for you?"

Cautiously, R' Kahan identified himself and his cause, wondering if it would have been better merely to set up a time for a meeting face-to-face. Much to his surprise, Hendon replied with an almost apologetic note in his voice.

"You know, Rabbi," the man said slowly, "I really owe you an apology. I know you've been trying to reach me for years, and it just never works out. What if you meet me in the lobby of the Hyatt tomorrow morning at ten? We could have a good, long talk, and take things from there."

R' Kahan could hardly believe it. "I'll be there," he managed to say. "Don't worry."

The next morning found R' Kahan pacing the ornate, marble lobby of the Hyatt well before ten o'clock. Finally, a few minutes after the appointed hour, a tall, athletic-looking man sauntered through the glass doors of the main entrance and approached.

"Greetings, Rabbi," Hendon said in his lazy drawl. "Sam Hendon's the name. Let's sit down and get to business."

The two men sat down on a velvet-upholstered sofa. R' Kahan described his *yeshivah* to Hendon and spoke about the importance of Torah education and the great responsibility of contributing to its support. Hendon listened attentively, asking intelligent questions from time to time. The minutes stretched out to half an hour, then longer. Finally, R' Kahan mustered enough courage to ask Hendon a question he had been wondering about for a long, long time.

"Mr. Hendon," he said tentatively. "You are the president of a company and you deal with many, many people. If anyone has their finger on the pulse of Harristown, it would be you."

Hendon chuckled. "And what diagnosis are you looking for?"

"As you know, I have been coming here to Harristown for several years. I also do some fundraising in Overton, your sister city. There are many similarities between Overton and Harristown: your Jewish communities are comprised of the same type of people, for example, and I would imagine that the average income is about the same, too. That being the case, could you explain to me why the people of Overton are so much more charitable than the people here in Harristown?"

Hendon froze. Watching him, R' Kahan wished there was some way he could snatch the question back. Antagonizing or insulting Hendon would certainly be the last way to convince him to make a donation.

"Rabbi," he finally whispered in a soft, child-like voice. "Rabbi, I'm so ashamed. I'm ashamed of myself and my city." He swallowed. "What will I say to my Maker when I pass away?" His voice broke, and he buried his face in his hands while he burst out in open sobs.

R' Kahan, astonished beyond belief, sat quietly and waited. Hendon's words had sounded almost like a *Yom Kippur* confession. What would be the final outcome?

After several moments, Hendon partially composed himself. In a trembling voice, he said, "Rabbi, whatever amount of money you ask, I'll give it to you. I—I want to redeem my community from this embarrassment..." Tears overflowed his eyes as he broke down once more.

R' Kahan softly suggested a figure. Hendon pulled out his checkbook and wrote out a check for the full amount.

As R' Kahan accepted the precious check, he felt a great sense of awe for this simple Jew who had willingly shouldered the shame of his community and opened his heart to the *mitzvah* of *tzedakah*.

Long-Term Success

There are those who expend great effort in bringing others closer to Torah. While the results in some cases are often seen immediately, other times the outcome is only recognizable after a long period of time.

Mr. Ernest Freundlich lives in Wilkes-Barre, Pennsylvania. The Jewish community is not a large one, but the Orthodox Jews were a close-knit, friendly group. He has a jewelry store not far from his home and leads a busy and contented life.

One day, a young man sporting an Afro hairdo and a single earring entered his store. Mr. Freundlich eyed him warily. There were any number of young gentiles dressed in similar fashion living in Wilkes-Barre, especially since there was a prominent Protestant parochial school nearby. Most of the students, however, did not frequent his jewelry shop. Mr. Freundlich wondered what the young man wanted.

He didn't have to wonder for long. The young man approached the counter with a friendly smile and said, "Hello there! Are you Mr. Freundlich?"

"Yes," Mr. Freundlich answered cautiously.

The young man's smile grew wider as he put out a hand. "Pleased to meet you. I'm Jeffrey Samson*, your cousin from Texas."

Mr. Freundlich shook Jeffrey's hand in a daze. His cousin! He had a cousin that looked like this?!

As he offered Jeffrey a chair, Mr. Freundlich tried to put the pieces of the puzzle together. He knew he had an irreligious cousin living in Houston, Texas, who had emigrated from Europe and succumbed to the easy temptations of American life. Jeffrey must be his cousin's son. But what was he doing here?

"What brings you to Wilkes-Barre?" he asked.

---

* *Names are fictitious.*

Jeffrey waved a casual hand. "Oh, I graduated elementary school last June. I started going to the parochial school here a few weeks back. My father told me that we've got this cousin right here in town, and that I should be sure to look you up." He gave an easy grin. "The first month or so was pretty hectic, but I finally managed to get away. So here I am!"

As the conversation continued, Mr. Freundlich learned a little more. Jeffrey's family had no connection with *Yiddishkeit* whatsoever. Jeffrey and his siblings had all attended the local public school and knew nothing about their precious heritage. Faced with the hollow emptiness of their ignorance in *Yiddishkeit*, the family had put all their emphasis on secular education instead, encouraging the children to attend college.

With the excellent reputation of the parochial school in Wilkes-Barre, it was hardly surprising that Jeffrey had chosen to go there. What *was* surprising was his apparent interest in his religious relatives. Perhaps, Mr. Freundlich thought hopefully, he could turn that interest to Jeffrey's advantage.

"If you're here in the school, you ought to come and meet the rest of my family," he suggested carefully. "How about coming over for a meal one Sabbath?"

Jeffrey's eyes lit up. "That would be great," he said enthusiastically. "The food on campus is pretty lousy. It would be super to have a real home-cooked meal for a change."

Mr. Freundlich suppressed a smile. It might not have been the best of motives, but it was a start. "In that case, you'll really love my wife's cooking," he assured the young man. "How about if you meet me in synagogue and we'll walk over to my house together afterwards?"

"That makes sense," Jeffrey agreed. "It'll probably be easier to find the synagogue than your house. I'll see you Saturday morning, then. Thanks a lot!"

With a smile and a wave, Jeffrey was gone. Mr. Freundlich sat down heavily in a chair, wondering what his wife would say when she saw what Jeffrey looked like.

That *Shabbos* morning, towards the end of *davening*, Jeffrey entered the *shul*, spotted Mr. Freundlich, and made his way down the aisle to sit down next to his older cousin. Heads turned in astonishment at the sight of Jeffrey's huge Afro and single earring. After a moment, most of the people tried to return their attention to the *davening*, but many couldn't help staring incredulously at the young man sitting next to Mr. Freundlich. Such attire was not a common sight in *shul*, to say the least!

Mr. Freundlich, however, behaved as if Jeffrey's way of dress was perfectly normal. He introduced him to several members of the *shul* as they made their way outside, then walked home with him, chatting in a pleasant fashion.

Mrs. Freundlich had received ample warning from her husband and met Jeffrey with only a startled blink. She graciously invited Jeffrey to sit down at the table and served her hot delicious meal.

The *Shabbos* meal was warm and friendly. The Freundlichs discussed many Jewish topics with Jeffrey, who responded with open curiosity. Even after *Birkas Hamazon*, Jeffrey remained for some time, engrossed in intriguing conversation. It was with clear reluctance that he finally took his leave, assuring his cousins that he would be back as soon as possible.

After that, Jeffrey was a frequent *Shabbos* visitor in the Freundlich home. His interest in *Yiddishkeit* grew steadily. One *Shabbos* afternoon, as they all sat on the couch in the living room, Mr. Freundlich decided it was time for the next step. "You know, Jeffrey, I was speaking to one of the rabbis from the day school here," he began. "I mentioned your name to him."

"Oh, yes?" Jeffrey said.

"Yes. I told him a little about you, and he said he'd be glad to spend some time learning some of the laws of *tefillin* with you." Mr. Freundlich took a deep breath. "Do you think you'd be interested?"

Jeffrey looked at his older cousin for a long moment. "I'll have to think about it," he said at last.

"Of course," Mr. Freundlich said quickly. "I can understand that."

The rest of the afternoon was stilted and slightly uncomfortable. Jeffrey seemed preoccupied as he thanked Mrs. Freundlich for the delicious meal and pleasant company. The Freundlichs stood in the doorway and watched as Jeffrey walked slowly down the block back to school.

"Do you think he'll accept the offer?" Mr. Freundlich wondered aloud.

His wife shrugged. "We'll just have to wait and see, I suppose."

Unfortunately, Jeffrey never came back to the Freundlich home. The Freundlichs were distressed at the thought that they might have pushed too far and too fast, frightening the young man away.

A few years later, Mr. and Mrs. Sam Berl*, residents of Wilkes-Barre who *davened* at the same *shul* as the Freundlichs, traveled to Eretz Yisrael for a two-week visit. During their stay, they went to a Jerusalem restaurant one evening for dinner. As they seated themselves and began to peruse the

---

* *Name is fictitious.*

menu, their waiter, a man with a beard, *payos* and *tzitzis* flying at his sides, approached. Mr. Berl was pleased to see that the waiter was a *yeshivah* boy, who was no doubt earning some money during the summer break.

"Good evening," the waiter said pleasantly. Then he took a closer look at Mr. Berl and exclaimed, "*Sholom aleichem,* Mr. Berl! Welcome to Eretz Yisrael."

Mr. Berl stared at the young man in astonishment. How did this waiter know his name? He'd never even met him before. "Ah, do I know you?" he stammered.

The waiter grinned. "I guess you don't recognize me."

"Should I?" Mr. Berl stared at the waiter's face, his mind racing frantically as he tried to place the young man. Was he a distant relative? Someone he'd met once on a trip to New York?

The waiter chuckled. "No, I guess it would be a little difficult. I'm Jeffrey. Remember? I used to sit next to Mr. Ernest Freundlich, my cousin, in *shul*. Your seat was right in front of mine."

Mr. Berl blinked, his mind going back to the events that had taken place a few years earlier. *This* was the boy that had shocked the members of the *shul* by showing up with an Afro haircut and a single earring? "Of course. I remember you now," he said finally with an apologetic smile. "I'm glad to see you've become a *ben Torah.*"

Jeffrey nodded. "Yes, I came to tour Israel and I joined a *yeshivah.*" He smiled. "I'm finally right where I belong."

The evening passed pleasantly. As the Berl's finished their meal and prepared to pay, Jeffrey approached Mr. Berl once more. "Would you do me a favor? When you get back to Wilkes-Barre, please send Mr. Freundlich and his wife my very best regards. Tell them I owe them everything. They're the ones who put the spark in me that made me *frum.*"

Mr. Berl smiled broadly and shook Jeffrey by the hand. "I'll pass on the message," he assured him. "I'll be proud to!"

Two years later, Mr. Freundlich received an invitation in the mail to a wedding in Israel. Jeffrey was getting married to a *religious* girl. On the back of the invitation, Jeffrey wrote, "I'll never forget the *chesed* you and your wife did for me by always inviting me to *Shabbos* meals and introducing me to *Yiddishkeit*. The love and concern your family showed me helped bring me back to being a true Jew. I hope you will come to Eretz Yisrael one day and grant me the opportunity to repay a little of the *chesed* you've always done for me."

Mr. Freundlich and his wife marvelled over the invitation. They'd thought that their efforts with Jeffrey had failed, but here was ample proof that in the long run, they'd succeeded.

Jeffrey wasn't content with just having a family of his own. With his influence, his two sisters have also returned to *Yiddishkeit* and are raising *frum* families of their own. The seed planted by the Freundlichs of Wilkes-Barre so long ago has flowered and still continues to grow.

Designated Livelihood

Rav Moshe Heschel, the son of the revered Kopicznitzer Rebbe, Rav Avraham Yehoshua Heschel, was the successor to his father's rabbonus after the rebbe's petirah. The following story, which took place before Rav Moshele had taken his father's position, clearly demonstrates Rav Moshele's suitability in continuing the Kopicznitzer dynasty.

To support his family, R' Moshele was in the diamond business. One morning, as he was on his way to work, he met R' Yitzchak Brandwein on the street. R' Moshele noticed that his friend looked very uneasy.

"What's the matter, Yitzchak?" he asked him.

R' Yitzchak gave a deep sigh. "I just started working in diamonds. I have been knocking on doors for several days, but I haven't made any money. You know, the key to this business is contacts. I need names of buyers and sellers, and I don't have any leads. So I've been getting nowhere."

R' Moshele noticed the look of desperation in R' Yitzchak's eyes. He quietly took a small notebook out of his pocket. "I just may be able to help you, Yitzchak. I have a list here of people who are both buyers and sellers of diamonds. Why don't you give them a try?"

R' Yitzchak took the list with a feeling of renewed hope. He started making a few calls, and with Hashem's help, his business began to take off. After a few sales, R' Yitzchak felt confident that he would be able to continue making a living.

Several days later, R' Yitzchak once again met R' Moshele in the street.

"*Nu*, Yitzchak," R' Moshele asked him, "how's it going?"

"*Baruch Hashem*," R' Yitzchak said gratefully. "I've managed to make a few sales, and things are looking up.

"But there's one thing I wanted to ask you. You know, I didn't go into this business blindly. I spoke to many people who were already diamond dealers, and they gave me many helpful suggestions. No one, however, offered me their list of contacts. After all, to do so would be giving away their livelihood to someone else!

"So why did you give me your list of names? You actually gave me your *parnassah*! Why did you do this for me?"

R' Moshele smiled. "Yitzchak, *gloib mir, vos iz mir ungeshribben, veste mir nisht tzinemen.* Believe me, you won't take away what I am destined to have."

R' Yitzchak continued on his way with a powerful lesson about the trust and faith we must have in Hashem, that *He* is our true provider.

ADMONISHMENT WITH LOVE

Recalling the revered Kopicznitzer Rebbe, Rav Avraham Yehoshua Heschel (1887-1963), brings to mind the pure and soft speech that always emanated from the rebbe's lips. One particular story, related by R' Yaakov Greenwald, took place back in the early days on the lower East Side, when the rebbe lived on Henry Street.

Every *Shabbos* morning, the *rebbe* would make his way down to the *mikveh* on East Broadway, where he would immerse himself before *davening*. One *Shabbos*, the *rebbe* noticed two non-religious Jews standing on the street, smoking cigarettes.

The *rebbe*, whose *ahavas Yisrael* was legendary, could not let himself pass without sharing his concern. He approached them cautiously and began to speak in a soft and gentle tone.

"Good *Shabbos, yidden.*"

"Good *Shabbos, rebbe*," they respectfully replied.

"May I ask you a question?" the *rebbe* said gently.

"Of course."

"The *Shabbos* is such a holy day, and you are such fine Jews. Why are you smoking on this holy day?"

The two men looked at each other for a moment. Then one of them turned back to the *rebbe*. "*Rebbe*, do you know what they say in America?" He paused for a moment, then continued. "Mind your own business!"

The *rebbe*, unfazed, continued to smile. Again he asked politely, "May I ask you another question?"

"Sure, go ahead."

The *rebbe* pointed to the cars going by on East Broadway. "This is a busy street, with many cars going by. Tell me, if you saw a car hit a person, and the person was lying there bleeding heavily, would you say, 'mind your own business'?"

"Of course not, *rebbe*! The man is lying there, bleeding to death. Of course we would help him."

"Well, it is the same situation here. I see two fine Jews standing on the street, with their souls bleeding to death. How can you tell me to mind my own business? Can you blame me for wanting to help them?"

The two men immediately threw the cigarettes away. "*Rebbe*, we promise not to smoke on *Shabbos* again!"

And every *Shabbos* when the *rebbe* went to the *mikveh*, he was greeted by these two men with a "Good *Shabbos*, *rebbe*" — and a friendly, "See, we aren't smoking on *Shabbos*!"

SAGACIOUS REBUKE

The following story was related by Rav Moshe Aaron Stern, mashgiach of Yeshivah Kaminetz in Yerushalayim and a grandson of Reb Yaakov Yosef Herman.

The great *tzaddik*, Rav Aryeh Levin, was known for the way he shared the pain of anyone in distress. Indeed, R' Aryeh attended every funeral he heard about, and he often gave a heartfelt eulogy. What was not as well known, however, was how R' Aryeh also loved to share in another's *simchah*—whether he knew him or not.

One *Shabbos* morning, R' Moshe Aaron Stern had *davened* at daybreak in his grandfather's *minyan* and was on his way to attend a *bar-mitzvah kiddush*. As he walked along Rechov Haneviim, he met R' Aryeh.

"Good *Shabbos*," R' Aryeh hailed him. "Where are you off to?"

"I'm going to a *bar-mitzvah*," R' Moshe Aaron told him.

"Fine," R' Aryeh said cheerfully. "Let's go together."

The two of them were walking together on the deserted street, talking in learning, when R' Moshe Aaron noticed a man walking toward them. The man bearing down on them was at least six feet tall, with shoulders and muscles to match—and he had a cigarette dangling from his mouth.

R' Moshe Aaron began to feel a little nervous. He knew that R' Aryeh would give the man his usual admonishment for desecrating the *Shabbos*. But this fellow didn't look as if he were willing to take anything from anybody. And if he did get mad, he would probably take it out on R' Moshe Aaron. After all, no one would start up with the saintly-looking R' Aryeh.

Sure enough, as they drew close to the man, R' Aryeh turned to him and said softly, "It is *Shabbos* today, and it is prohibited to smoke."

The man gave a start of surprise. His eyes glinted with anger for a moment, but then he controlled himself and said firmly, "I am not a Jew."

"You are a Jew," R' Aryeh said lovingly. "You are my

brother. I am only telling you not to smoke because I love you, and I am concerned for you."

The man stared at R' Aryeh in astonishment. Slowly, his angry look melted away, and he looked down at the ground in confusion.

"Rebbe, do you want me to put the cigarette out?" he asked quietly.

"No," R' Aryeh said with a smile. "That, too, is not allowed. Just put it down on the ground and leave it there."

The man took the cigarette out of his mouth and laid it carefully on the ground. Then he looked back at R' Aryeh.

"*Rebbe*, I want you to know that people have been giving me admonishment all of my life. But I never listened to them, because they really weren't doing it for my good—they were only interested in insulting me. You were different, though. I could tell that your words truly came from the heart.

"*Rebbe*, I won't tell you that I'll start keeping *Shabbos* from now on. But I will keep this *Shabbos*. Tell me when nightfall is, and I will behave in the spirit of *Shabbos* until then."

R' Aryeh told him when *Shabbos* was due to be over, then wished him well, and the man went on his way.

R' Moshe Aaron and R' Aryeh continued on to the *barmitzvah*. But R' Moshe Aaron now had a special awareness of the serenity of *Shabbos*—as well as a lesson in how to truly admonish a fellow Jew.

4
NOBLE ATTRIBUTES

A Pearl to Remember
■ ■ ■
Marooned in Maine
■ ■ ■
A Run for It
■ ■ ■
Anything for a Mother
■ ■ ■
Tzedakah Incognito
■ ■ ■

4
Noble Attributes

A PEARL TO REMEMBER

Events that occur in one's life tend to be forgotten as the years go by. In the following story, a kindness done many years before was truly remembered and appreciated.

As a dynamic young man in the early 1960's, Zev Feit was a hard worker who brought home a good paycheck every week. With his mother's birthday just around the corner, Zev decided to spend part of his savings on a special present for her. He considered the matter for some time before finally settling on a necklace as the perfect gift.

Zev called Baruch, a family friend, and asked him for advice. "I don't know the first thing about jewelry, but I want to get my mother something really nice. Do me a favor and find me a good, honest dealer. I need someone I can trust or I'll really be taken for a ride."

Baruch thought it over for a moment. "I know just the person for you, Zev. Give me a day or two and I'll arrange everything."

A few days later, Baruch personally escorted Zev to a tiny shop where an elderly Polish Jew sat behind a narrow counter. Baruch introduced Zev to the dealer and explained that the young man wanted to purchase a birthday gift for his mother.

"Zev is a good friend of mine," Baruch stressed. "Please treat him the same way you would treat me."

The elderly dealer nodded reassuringly, and Baruch gave Zev an encouraging pat on the shoulder and left.

"Well, young man," the old man began. "You want to buy a necklace for your mother. How much do you want to spend?"

"A few hundred dollars," Zev said cautiously. "Can you show me some necklaces in that price range?"

The dealer pulled out several trays of pearl necklaces. "Here. These necklaces cost two hundred fifty dollars, these four hundred, these three hundred . . ."

Zev helplessly eyed the strings of pearls. "I - I really don't understand the difference between them. Could you please explain?"

Patiently, the dealer pointed out the differences in colors and sizes, explaining why one type of pearl was considered more valuable than another. As the "lesson" continued, the old man asked Zev about his family background.

"It isn't every young man who wants to buy a necklace for his mother," he commented. "What is your family name? Where are you from?"

"My full name is Zev Feit," Zev replied. "I was brought up here in America. But my mother is originally from Poland, from Galicia, from the city of Sanok."

The dealer stopped fiddling with the pearls and looked up at Zev. "What was your mother's maiden name?"

"Rivka Berger," answered Zev. "Her mother was Sarah Berger."

The dealer studied him for another long moment. "So you are buying this pearl necklace for Sarah Berger's daughter?"

"Well, yes," Zev said, puzzled. "But—"

Without another word, the dealer suddenly snatched up the trays of pearls and thrust them out of sight beneath the counter.

"Hey, wait a minute!" Zev protested. "I haven't decided which necklace to buy."

"I cannot sell you any of these," the dealer said firmly. He turned and disappeared through a door at the back of the store. Zev stood there, bewildered by the sudden change of events. Why wouldn't this elderly Jew sell him a pearl necklace for his mother?

Moments later, the dealer came marching back, holding a single necklace in his hand. "Here," he said, laying the necklace on the counter. "I will sell you this one. It costs five hundred dollars."

"But—but —" Zev sputtered. "What about the other necklaces? Why do you want me to buy this one?"

The dealer shook his head. "No, this one. I will sell you only these pearls. They cost five hundred dollars."

"I don't understand," Zev said, upset. "You told Baruch you would treat me well, but you—"

"I *am* treating you well," the old Jew interrupted. "I assure you. I am treating you just as I would Reb Baruch, and I am telling you to buy these pearls. Believe me, they are perfect for your mother."

Zev looked down at the string of pearls in the dealer's

hand. To his untrained eye, they seemed practically identical to the other necklaces now hidden out of sight beneath the counter. Why should he pay five hundred dollars for this particular necklace? On the other hand, he trusted Baruch, and Baruch evidently believed that this Jew was an honest, trustworthy dealer. Zev decided to purchase the necklace.

A few days later, Zev proudly gave his mother the birthday present he had so carefully chosen for her. Mrs. Feit was both delighted and astonished by her gift.

"They're beautiful, Zev," she said. "But you didn't have to do this. I'm sure you paid too much for them. How much did they cost?"

Zev refused to tell his mother how much he had spent, saying only that he had purchased the necklace through Baruch. "Don't worry. I know I got a good deal, and I'm glad I was able to do it."

Mrs. Feit cherished her precious birthday gift, saving the long string of pearls only for the most special occasions. When she was not wearing them, she kept them hidden in a small box behind the dressing table in her bedroom.

Fifteen years passed. The pearl necklace appeared at Zev's wedding and at other special family affairs, but the bizarre tale of the Polish dealer had been long since forgotten.

Events took a new turn when the mirror on the dressing table fell down and crashed right onto the little box containing the pearl necklace. While the pearls themselves were undamaged, the string snapped in two. The impact sent the pearls flying all over the room, rolling into corners and underneath chairs.

Upset, Mrs. Feit carefully gathered all the pearls together and took them to a jeweller she knew, asking him to arrange to have the necklace restrung. The jeweller promised Zev's mother he would take care of it and sent the pearls to a fellow dealer to do the job.

When the man brought the restrung necklace back to the jeweller, he commented, "You don't often send me jewelry of this quality. I didn't know that you had such rich customers."

"What do you mean?" the jeweller demanded. "My customer isn't rich."

"Yeah?" The man looked skeptical. "So what's she doing with a pearl necklace worth over six thousand dollars?"

The jeweller was astonished. "It can't be!" he blurted. "It's impossible. The customer is a friend of mine. She's not rich at all."

The man shrugged. "I don't know about that, but I do know pearls, and I would value these at over six thousand dollars."

The jeweller called Mrs. Feit on the telephone. "How can you wear such expensive pearls?" he asked her. "You never struck me as the showy type."

"What are you talking about?" Mrs. Feit asked, mystified. "Are my pearls ready or not?"

"Yes, yes, they're all ready. You can come down and get them."

When Mrs. Feit arrived at the shop, the jeweller was waiting impatiently. He waved the pearls at her. "This necklace is worth over six thousand dollars! How can you walk around with pearls like this?"

Zev's mother was speechless. Six thousand dollars! It was impossible. Could her son have really paid so much money all those years ago for a birthday gift?

"I can't explain it," she mumbled. She paid the jeweller for restringing the pearls and gingerly carried the necklace home. She carefully locked the door before calling up Zev and indignantly demanding why he had spent so much money on her.

"But I didn't," Zev protested.

"You must have," Mrs. Feit asserted. "The jeweller said my pearls are worth six thousand dollars. How could you spend so much money on a necklace?"

"I didn't," Zev insisted. "I paid five hundred dollars, that's all. If the dealer sold me a six-thousand-dollar necklace for five hundred dollars . . . Look, talk to Baruch. He introduced me to the dealer in the first place. Maybe he can explain it."

Mrs. Feit did call Baruch, but Baruch was unable to explain why an old Polish Jew had sold Zev such a valuable string of pearls for such a low price.

"Well, can you ask him?" Mrs. Feit pressed.

"Mr. Mikovsky* died many years ago," Baruch said regretfully. "I wish I had an explanation for you, but there's no way we'll ever find out now."

Baruch was wrong. A few months later, Mrs. Feit was talking to her older sister and related the entire story. "Imagine, Zev paid five hundred dollars for a pearl necklace that's valued at over six thousand! Why should this Mr. Mikovsky do such a thing?"

"Mikovsky," her sister repeated thoughtfully. "Mikovsky . . . Oh, yes, of course! Listen, Rivka. I think I have the explanation.

"By the time you were born, the czars were no longer in power, but I can still remember how the czar would send soldiers into town to round up the young Jewish children and conscript them into the army. We all knew that it was a death sentence to these young boys. Richer families were

---

*Name is fictitious.

able to bribe the soldiers into leaving their children alone, but the poorer families in town were forced to try to hide their children or run away before they could be caught.

"During one of these roundups, a young boy named Mikovsky came scratching at our door in the middle of the night. He told our parents that the soldiers were after him and begged them to help him hide. It was dangerous, but our parents took him into the house and hid him in the cellar, feeding him and guarding him until the soldiers had left town in search of other victims.

"They never found Mikovsky. He left our home when it was safe, and the last news we heard of him was that he had managed to escape to America. That must be the explanation, Rivka. The old Polish dealer was none other than the same boy that our parents saved from forced conscription into the army."

Mrs. Feit called Zev and excitedly told him the story. "What do you think, Zev? Could this possibly be the answer?"

Zev thought back, trying to remember an incident that had taken place fifteen years before. "Yes. Yes, that must be it! I remember, he asked me about our family. I told him your maiden name, and he very carefully asked if I was buying the necklace for Sarah Berger's daughter. He must have recognized the name and felt that this was his chance to repay an old debt of gratitude. No other explanation makes sense."

Zev's mother treasured the precious pearls for the rest of her life, awed at the tremendous *hakaras hatov* inherent in their value. After her passing, the pearls were given to Zev's daughter Sarah, named after the grandmother who had saved Mikovsky's life so many decades before.

MAROONED IN MAINE

The Gemara relates the story of Dama ben Nesina, a gentile, as an example of the extent to which one is required to honor one's parents. There are those that explain that the Gemara deliberately uses Dama ben Nesina to illustrate kibud av v'em in order to teach us that we are required to learn good traits from everyone, even non-Jews.

In the summer of 1988, R' Moshe Chaim Pollak and his family travelled to New Hampshire and Maine for their summer vacation. The trip was a pleasant one, as the children enjoyed the beautiful mountains and striking scenery of Acadia National Park. All too soon, however, it was time to turn the car around and head for home.

The Pollaks drove for several hours before R' Pollak realized that he was having some difficulty controlling the steering. Alarmed, he pulled to the side of the road and turned off the motor. He lifted the hood and poked inside for a few minutes, but he was unable to locate the problem.

"Any luck?" Mrs. Pollak called as her husband closed the hood.

R' Pollak shook his head and got back into the car. "I can't tell what's wrong. We'd better drive slowly to the next available exit and find a mechanic to fix the car."

Unfortunately, this plan proved to be untenable. Despite R' Pollak's best efforts, the car wouldn't start at all.

The Pollaks looked at each other, then glanced at the children in the back seat. It was already close to seven o'clock, and it would soon be dark. They didn't have AAA, so they couldn't call for assistance. Even if they found a public phone somewhere along the highway, most garages would probably be closed for the night. Were they stranded on the road until morning?

As they sat there, going over their options, a pick-up truck drove past, then braked and veered to the side of the road just ahead of them.

"Oh, good," Mrs. Pollak said with relief. "Now we can get help."

Her husband nodded and began to get out of the car to greet their rescuer. He froze in mid-motion as the driver of the pick-up swung out of the cab and walked toward them.

The huge, bare-chested man sported a fiery red beard and a wicked-looking scar across his cheek. As he came closer, the Pollaks exchanged glances of pure terror. Would this giant of a man help them, or did he have something else in mind?

"Hello, there," the man boomed. He engulfed R' Pollak's hand in his huge palm and shook it vigorously. "Mackentire's the name, John Mackentire."

"Pollak," R' Pollak mumbled.

"Having a spot of trouble, eh?" He glanced at the back seat and beamed. His smile sent a shiver up R' Pollak's spine. "I see you've got your kids with you. Well then, is there any way I can help you out?"

"Ah, I can't get the car started," R' Pollak stammered. "Really, all I need is a phone so I can call for help."

"That's no problem," Mackentire said expansively. "Hop into the cab, and I'll drive you to the nearest phone."

R' Pollak looked back at his wife. Mrs. Pollak gulped, then put on a brave smile and nodded. It would surely be better for her husband to go with Mackentire and get him as far away from the rest of the family as possible!

"I'll be back as soon as I can," he promised her, giving a reassuring smile to his children for good measure. "I'll find a motel where we can spend the night, and then we'll get the car fixed in the morning."

"Oh, you don't need to bother with that," Mackentire interjected. "Why waste money on a motel? You folks can be put up at my house. I live only half an hour away from here."

"Thanks, but no," R' Pollak said quickly and firmly. "We'll be more comfortable in a motel." Go to this man's house? Certainly not!

"Well, if you're sure . . ." Mackentire walked back to the pick-up truck without looking back to see if the other man was following him. "There's a motel not too far away. There's a public phone outside, but you might as well try out the motel first."

"Thank you," R' Pollak said as he clambered into the back of the truck. "We really appreciate it."

The truck rumbled back onto the road and drove off. R' Pollak craned his neck to look back at his car and his family huddled inside. He hoped Mackentire wasn't planning anything so he'd be able to get back to his wife and children as soon as possible.

The motel seemed clean enough, but the place was booked solid. "Sorry, sir," the receptionist said apologetically. "We get a lot of vacationers at this time of year. Most people make reservations ahead of time."

R' Pollak's heart sank. "Uh, are there any other motels in the neighborhood?"

The receptionist gave him the names of two other motels within a twenty-minute radius. He scurried across the lobby to use the public phone. The calls didn't take long; both motels had the same answer. "We're sorry, sir, but we're booked full tonight."

As he hung up the phone for the second time, Mackentire tapped him on the shoulder. R' Pollak jumped. It felt more like a hammer than a finger.

"Look," Mackentire said reasonably. "You folks are stuck. Why don't you come sleep at my place? My wife's a nurse, but she's not home right now. I've got the place to myself. I have a kid just about the same age as yours, and I'd really like to do you folks a good turn."

R' Pollak looked Mackentire up and down. The red-bearded giant still looked more like a wild man than a civilized stranger, but he was beginning to realize that they had little choice. With twilight darkening the sky, their only options seemed to be spending the night huddled in the car or in Mackentire's home.

He wasn't sure which choice was worse. "Let's go back to the car," he said finally. "I'll discuss it with my wife."

Mackentire drove him back to where the stalled car was parked, chatting happily all the while. "I really hope your wife will agree to come stay by my house tonight. I'm telling you, you'll really enjoy it. I built the house myself. Maine is one of the most beautiful areas in the world, and I've got a view that you've got to see to believe!"

R' Pollak nodded noncommittally and made vague comments in reply. He was too busy worrying about his wife's reaction to work up any enthusiasm for the situation, beautiful scenery or not.

They arrived at the car just as the sun vanished below the mountains. Mrs. Pollak scrambled out of the car as soon as the pick-up truck pulled to the side of the road.

"What happened?" she asked anxiously. "Did you find place in a motel?"

Her husband opened his mouth to speak, but Mackentire beat him to it. "I'm afraid not," he said cheerfully, "so I guess it would be best if you folks spent the night at my place."

Mrs. Pollak stared at him in shock. R' Pollak diplomatically pulled his wife to one side so they could talk in private.

"I am *not* going to spend the night in that man's house!" Mrs. Pollak hissed. "I'd rather stay here in the car. I don't trust him."

"I don't like it either," her husband admitted. "But look at this place. It's the middle of nowhere, and it's already night. It wouldn't be safe to stay here."

"I don't think it would be safe to stay with him, either," Mrs. Pollak muttered.

R' Pollak extended his hands. "There are no lights on the road, and this stretch of road is completely deserted. Did anyone else drive by while we were gone?"

"No," Mrs. Pollak admitted reluctantly.

Her husband shrugged. "So what choice do we have? This must be *min haShamayim*. We'll keep a careful eye on our host, that's all."

Mrs. Pollak finally agreed that her husband was right. He went back to Mackentire, who still stood waiting patiently by the side of his pick-up truck. "It looks like we'll be accepting your kind invitation," R' Pollak told him.

Mackentire's entire face lit up. His scar looked more livid than ever in the glare of the headlights. "Wonderful! I'm so glad to have guests."

"Yeah, right," R' Pollak mumbled to himself as he headed back to his car to help his wife transfer their children and their belongings to Mackentire's truck. He just hoped he was doing the right thing by agreeing to spend the night by this wild-looking stranger's home.

With the children settled in the back of the cab and the Pollaks squeezed onto the front bench with Mackentire, the truck lumbered off into the night. Mackentire kept up a steady stream of conversation, apparently without noticing the Pollaks' lack of response.

"Your kids will really love my place. Like I told you, it's

set right in the most gorgeous scenery in Maine. I chose the site myself. I just finished building it a couple of years ago. Right in the middle of the woods, no other houses around to disturb the peace and quiet..."

The Pollaks looked at each apprehensively as the truck whined up a steep mountain road. An isolated house wasn't their idea of an ideal situation.

Mackentire glanced at his passengers. "You know, I don't think I've ever met Jews before. You *are* Jews, aren't you?"

"Uh, yes," R' Pollak stammered.

"Religious?"

"Yes."

Mackentire nodded thoughtfully. "I'm religious too. I'm a Christian Scientist. I've always wanted to discuss religion with a Jew, but I never had the chance before."

"Discussion?" R' Pollak said weakly.

"Well, I've always wondered. Did you Jews really kill our lord?"

R' Pollak gulped. Stuck in a Christian's car, on their way to a house in the middle of nowhere, was not the best place for a philosophical discussion. "This isn't really the best time to talk about it," he said quickly and evasively. "I've had a really rough day, you know. Maybe we could save it for another time."

"Oh, sure. No problem." Mackentire lapsed into silence.

Mrs. Pollak looked back at her children. Where were they being taken? What would this Christian Scientist do to them?

After another quarter of an hour, the headlights shone on a house not too far ahead. As Mackentire pulled into the driveway, flood lights suddenly went on and a large dog began to bark violently.

"What's that?" Mrs. Pollak gasped.

"Security," Mackentire said cheerfully. "All alone out here, you've gotta be careful."

R' Pollak agreed entirely. He just wished he knew if they were being careful enough.

They climbed wearily out of the truck, plagued by anxiety and second thoughts. Staying in their broken-down car on the side of a darkened road suddenly seemed safer than entering the home of a Christian Scientist with who knew what intentions. As they entered the front hall of Mackentire's house, moose and bear heads mounted on the wall seemed to leap out at them. Mrs. Pollak instinctively gathered her children closer to her, wondering wildly if their heads would be mounted there, too.

Mackentire didn't seem to notice the Pollaks' apprehension. "Time for a little dinner," he offered. "What will you folks have?"

"I'm sorry," R' Pollak said carefully. "But as we said before, we're religious Jews. We have strict dietary laws. I'm afraid that we won't be able to eat anything."

"Hey, that's right. I've heard about that before." Mackentire scratched his head. "How about some juice, then? Or some milk for the kids?"

"Really, it's all right," R' Pollak said quickly. "We have our own food. All we really need is a place to sleep."

Mackentire escorted the Pollak family up a flight of stairs and showed them into a large room. "I can put your little one in a crib, if you'd like," he volunteered. "I'll bring it in here." Before the Pollaks could say a word, the huge man had gone into another room and come back dragging a portable crib with him. "There. That should do it."

"Yes, it should," Mrs. Pollak said faintly. "Thank you very much."

"Hey, it's no trouble at all. Sleep well!" Mackentire waved and went down the hall.

Sleep well. The Pollaks looked at each other. How were they going to sleep at all?

They got the children settled as best as they could. Untroubled by the same fears that plagued their parents, the children were soon fast asleep. The Pollaks sat on two chairs, conversing in whispers. Should they take turns staying up during the night to make sure that Mackentire didn't try to enter the room?

As they debated the issue, a sudden rumble sounded through the room. Mrs. Pollak choked back a scream. "What is it?" she gasped.

Her husband dashed over to the door and opened it slightly. The sound came again, even louder. He listened for a moment, then relaxed and turned to his wife with a grim smile. "It's Mackentire," he said succinctly. "He's just snoring."

"That's snoring? It sounds more like a truck motor!"

"Well, maybe it's for the best," R' Pollak pointed out. "There's no question that we know he's asleep. Let's try to get some rest ourselves. I'll leave the door open a crack so we can hear if the snoring stops."

The Pollaks, still apprehensive, settled down for the night. R' Pollak placed his wallet under his pillow for safekeeping. He had less than one hundred dollars with him, but it was all the money he had to get them home.

Despite his anxiety, R' Pollak was soon sound asleep. Mrs. Pollak spent some time listening to the loud snores emanating from Mackentire before she, too, fell asleep out of sheer exhaustion.

In the middle of the night, R' Pollak suddenly opened his eyes. The room was pitch dark. He had no idea what had awakened him. Then he felt it again—something touching his leg.

Galvanized with fear, he jumped wildly out of bed. "Who's there?" he screamed. "Where's the light switch?"

Mrs. Pollak, awakened by her husband's yell, scrambled away from the noise. "What is it? What's happening?"

R' Pollak's fumbling hand found the light switch and turned it on. Bright, comforting light flooded the room and revealed a tabby cat sitting placidly on his pillow.

"It was just a cat," he gasped, struggling to regain his composure. As if to add further reassurance, the sound of Mackentire's snores rumbled through the room, sounding louder than ever.

Mrs. Pollak laughed shakily. "We left the door open, remember? It must have gotten inside that way."

R' Pollak checked that his wallet was still safe, then shoved the cat out of the room and closed the door firmly. "Let's try to get back to sleep," he suggested, feeling foolish at being so frightened by a cat. "I don't think we have anything to worry about any more."

When he woke up again, bright sunshine was streaming through the windows. Looking out at the scenery, he felt a lurch of alarm: the house was built at the top of a thousand-foot cliff. Still, the scenery was every bit as beautiful as Mackentire had claimed. He spent several minutes marvelling at the beauty of Hashem's creation before he dressed and *davened*. *Shacharis* took on a fervent note as he thanked Hashem for helping them make it through the night.

A few hours later, Mackentire awoke. By that time, the entire Pollak family was dressed, *davened*, and fed. "Good morning," Mackentire said genially. "Did you folks sleep well?"

"Very," R' Pollak said dryly, thinking of the cat.

"I'm glad. Now, how about some breakfast?"

"We've already eaten," R' Pollak explained. "I'm sorry, but—"

"Oh, yeah, that's right. You can't eat my stuff. You know, I really respect you folks and the way you're so careful about your religion."

With the reassuring sunshine streaming through the windows, Mackentire was not the same frightening giant he had appeared to be the night before. R' Pollak felt himself relax. This Christian Scientist wasn't such a bad fellow after all.

Mackentire once again began to ask several questions about Judaism and Christianity. R' Pollak felt more equipped to answer his questions, but after several minutes, he interrupted the discussion.

"We'd really like to spend the day with you, but it would probably be best if we went back to the car and found ourselves a mechanic." He smiled apologetically. "It's not that we don't appreciate your generous hospitality, but I'd really like to get the children back home."

"I understand," Mackentire assured him. "Let's pile back into the truck, and we'll see what we can do."

This time, the trip through the woods was an enjoyable experience. Friendly sunshine peeked through the trees, and Mackentire pointed out several animals as they drove. The Pollaks sat back and enjoyed the beautiful view of the mountains as they drove back down the steep road they had climbed the night before.

When they got back to the car, R' Pollak began to transfer their belongings back into the trunk. Meanwhile, Mackentire tried to start the car. Nothing happened.

"Did you take a look under the hood?" he asked.

"Yes, but I wasn't able to figure it out," R' Pollak explained. "I know my way around cars, but I'm not exactly an expert mechanic."

"Well, I am." Mackentire got out of the car and lifted the hood. "I used to work for a car mechanic myself." He poked around for a few moments, then looked up. "It's your starter. All we have to do is pick up a new one, and your car will be just fine."

R' Pollak hesitated. If Mackentire was right, it would save a lot of time. But what if he was wrong? The Pollaks had less than a hundred dollars with them, and a starter was expensive. Could they afford to take such a risk?

"Well, come on," Mackentire urged, starting back toward the truck. "I'll run you into town, and we'll pick up a starter."

R' Pollak sighed and followed Mackentire to the truck. He really had no choice.

They drove to an auto store and purchased a starter. Pollak winced as he took forty dollars out of his wallet and paid for their purchase. If Mackentire was wrong . . .

But he wasn't. When they got back to the car, Mackentire installed the starter himself before getting into the car once more and turning the key into the ignition. The car started immediately. R' Pollak grinned with relief as the motor purred into action.

"Well done!" he exclaimed, shaking Mackentire's hand gratefully. Mackentire beamed with delight and pumped his hand back. Pollak got his hand back with an effort, then began packing his family into the car.

When everything was settled and they were ready to start their journey back home, R' Pollak turned to Mackentire and said, "We really can't thank you enough. We appreciate everything you've done for us. Won't you let us pay you for your hospitality? We were ready to pay for a motel, after all."

Mackentire shook his head vigorously. "I won't hear of it," he said firmly. "Certainly not. Putting up you folks for the night was my good deed, and I can't take money for that."

"Well, at least let me pay you for fixing the car," R' Pollak urged.

Mackentire frowned, then shrugged. "All right. I'll let you pay me for the labor to get your car started, but I won't take money for my hospitality."

After a few minutes more of discussion, R' Pollak paid Mackentire twenty-five dollars for his labor and expertise. Then they shook hands once more before getting into their respective vehicles and driving off in opposite directions. The Pollaks' children waved good-bye. Mackentire waved back.

As the pick-up truck dwindled in his rear-view mirror, R' Pollak shook his head in bemusement at their incredible experience. *Baruch Hashem*, the whole incident had turned out well, but he was struck with a sobering thought: if a Christian was so willing to extend open hospitality to a complete stranger without thought of compensation, then surely he, as a religious Jew, must recognize the value of *hachnassas orchim* and the importance of performing *mitzvos* for their sake alone.

A RUN FOR IT

At times, living in accordance with one's noblest instincts is a difficult task. There are those who nevertheless overcome this and display sublime character traits even amidst the most pressing situations.

It was the day after *Yom Kippur*. R' Shmuel Spiegel and his wife were off to Detroit to spend *yom tov* with her family. The drive to Newark Airport usually took an hour, but a late start and unexpected traffic held them up. It was 4:05 by the time R' Shmuel pulled up at the terminal, with only fifteen minutes before their 4:20 flight was due to leave.

R' Shmuel left his wife and luggage at the terminal, then set off for the long term parking lot. He glanced at his watch with a sinking feeling. There was no way he would make it. It took at least five minutes to get to the parking lot. Then he would have to find a parking space, park the car, and get back to the terminal. The whole operation usually took at least twenty minutes. And he would still have to go all the way to the gate to check in for his flight!

R' Shmuel realized that there was no way he would make it. Still, he had to do his best. And so he floored the accelerator in an attempt to make it to the parking lot as quickly as possible.

All too soon, he was stopped by a red light. As he waited impatiently for the light to turn green, R' Shmuel noticed a police car in the lane right next to him.

"Just great," he moaned, as his hands tensed on the steering wheel. Now he would really have to be careful.

The light turned green, and R' Shmuel hit the gas. But one pedestrian hadn't been paying attention, and he stepped out into the street just as R' Shmuel's car surged forward.

R' Shmuel slammed on the brakes. The car stopped with a jerk, but it wasn't fast enough. The pedestrian flew up in the air and landed right on the windshield.

R' Shmuel froze in fright, but he breathed a sigh of relief

when the man rolled off the hood of his car and stood up, apparently unhurt. The man started screaming and yelling, but R' Shmuel had no time to waste. The police officer hadn't signalled to him, so R' Shmuel once again hit the accelerator, leaving the pedestrian yelling behind him.

Minutes later, he reached the parking lot. Miraculously, there was a space available right away. R' Shmuel parked the car, grabbed a few odds and ends and started running for the terminal. He glanced at his watch with a feeling of despair. There was no way he would make it.

Out of the corner of his eye, R' Shmuel saw a minivan cruising past. Suddenly the van went into reverse and began backing up to him. As the car drew level with him, the driver rolled down the window and beckoned R' Shmuel over.

R' Shmuel stared in shock. It was the man he had knocked over, just a few minutes before! What was he going to do to him?

"You seem to be in a big hurry!" the man called to him. "Maybe I can give you a lift?"

R' Shmuel couldn't believe what he was hearing. "Are you talking to me?"

"Yeah, sure, hop in! Just tell me where you need to go!"

In a daze, R' Shmuel got into the car. "I've got a flight to catch at terminal C," he told the smiling driver.

"No problem," the man said cheerfully.

As the van drove back the way he had just come, R' Shmuel kept giving the driver sidelong glances. What had caused the man to be so friendly? One thing was certain, though: it was only due to his benefactor that R' Shmuel was going to make his flight.

As the van pulled up in front of Terminal C, R' Shmuel got out and thanked the driver. "I wouldn't have made my flight without your help," he told him.

"It was my pleasure," the man told him. "But please, keep one thing in mind. It's the day after *Yom Kippur*, and you have to be careful not to hurt your fellow Jew."

It was then that R' Shmuel understood the man's kindness. Despite the clear differences between them, this man was still happy to go out of his way to help another Jew.

ANYTHING FOR A MOTHER

While everyone understands and appreciates the importance of honoring one's parents, many allow other aspects of their lives— personal honor, self-esteem, or even reluctance —to conflict with their obligation. In this story, Rabbi Aharon Weitz, Director of Echo Institute for Health, tells of a friend who did not let anything stand in his way when it came to truly honoring his mother.

Ben Freeman lives in the city of Los Angeles. As a young boy, his father died, leaving him and his mother to fend for themselves. Mother and son grew especially close in their joint struggle, until they were almost inseparable.

Years passed. Ben married and raised a family, but his mother remained a prime focus in his life. He would drop anything to take care of her or fulfill a particular request.

As the decades passed, their initial roles reversed themselves, as Mrs. Freeman became more frail and dependent on her son for assistance. By the time Ben's mother reached her nineties, her health had deteriorated, and she needed extensive medical attention. One day, when Ben took his mother for a checkup, the doctor called him aside and spoke to him privately.

"Your mother cannot live alone anymore," the doctor said seriously. "I think it would be best if you arranged for her to live in a nursing home."

"I can't do that!" Ben said, aghast. "Just leave my mother like that?"

"Your mother needs constant medical supervision," the doctor stressed again. "She would receive sufficient care in a nursing home. What other option do you have?"

Ben shook his head, determined. "As long as there's any other way to manage, I will," he declared. "My mother will move into my home. Then she won't be alone."

The doctor frowned. "You would have to arrange for constant nursing care and purchase expensive medical equipment."

"But can it be done?" Ben persisted.

"I suppose so," the doctor said thoughtfully. "But it'll be very difficult for you. Difficult, and expensive as well."

"That doesn't matter," Ben said in a quiet tone. "My mother is more important than money."

Mrs. Freeman moved in with her son's family. Ben spared no effort to arrange the best home medical care for his mother, including a nurse in constant attendance and expensive medical equipment. The costs were astronomical, but Ben wasn't troubled by the expense. What did money matter when it came to helping his mother?

The years went by. Mrs. Freeman remained in her son's home, surrounded by loving family and the best possible care in the time remaining to her before she passed away.

Ben was devastated by his mother's death. A major part of his life had been taken away. He took what little comfort he could from the knowledge that she had lived a long, happy, fruitful life. Subdued and shaken, he made preparations for his mother's funeral, including the arrangements for her burial in Israel.

Suddenly, Ben found himself faced with a terrible dilemma. His mother had specifically requested that she be buried in Israel, and Ben was ready to pay whatever costs necessary for the journey. Now, however, he found himself confronted with a California state law that he had never heard of before. According to the law, a body that is to be transported out of the state for burial must first be drained of blood and have chemical fluids substituted instead. Ben was horrified. How could he possibly fulfill his mother's last request?

Ben hurried over to the mortuary and asked to see the head mortician. In a few moments, the man appeared and courteously asked what he could do to help.

"It's about my mother, Mrs. Freeman," Ben began. "I want to have her buried in Israel."

"That should be no problem, sir," the mortician assured him. "Of course, we will have to drain the blood and—"

"But that's just it," Ben interrupted him. "I can't do that. Jewish law forbids it. The body of the deceased may not be tampered with in any way."

The mortician looked at him blankly. "This isn't Israel, sir," he said politely. "This is California. I'm afraid I have to follow the state law, not Jewish law. You understand, I'm sure."

"But I can't do it that way," Ben said desperately. "Surely there's some way to circumvent the law so that my mother can be buried in Israel."

The mortician looked at him with sympathy. "I'd like to help you. Really I would. But you see, I would lose my license if I don't comply with the law. If you want your mother buried in Israel, you'll have to allow me to replace her blood with chemical fluids."

Ben clenched his fists. "Look," he said finally. "I've spent every last penny I have in taking care of my mother. Now she's made this one last request, and I'm not going to let anything stop me from keeping it. All I have left is my house." He took a deep breath. "Skip the procedure, and my house is yours."

The mortician stood there for a full minute in silence, staring at Ben's anxious face. He had never met anyone before who was so willing to go to such lengths for his parent's honor. "I can see how much this means to you, Mr. Freeman," he said at last. "I'll do it for you. But I won't take your house."

Ben's mother was buried on Har Hamenuchos, according to *halachah*, with the respect that was due her.

The story does not end here. The people involved were so impressed with Ben's sincere respect for his mother and his willingness to sacrifice every last penny in her honor that arrangements were made for the issue to be reviewed in legislation. The State of California, after due consideration, decided to abolish the law. Thanks to one man's complete devotion to the *mitzvah* of *kibud eim*, California's state law no longer poses any difficulty for those concerned with *halachah*.

TZEDDAKAH INCOGNITO

Sometimes the mitzvah of giving tzeddakah is particularly meritorious, in accordance with the manner in which it is given. The following is a case in point.

When Binyomin travelled to Eretz Yisrael in the early 1970's to study in a *yeshivah*, he was eager to discover what life would be like in the holy city of Yerushalayim. He had never been to Eretz Yisrael before. How could he have imagined the many profound lessons he would absorb while he was there?

It did not take long for Binyomin to develop a tremendous respect for the Jews of Yerushalayim. Many of them lived frugally, with little money to call their own; others had so little that they literally did not know how to purchase food for their next meal. Nevertheless, these same Jews were full of faith in Hashem's ability to provide them with sustenance. Instead of worrying about money, these Jews devoted their days to Torah learning and *yiras shamayim*.

One afternoon, Binyomin missed his regular *minyan* for *Minchah* and went to the Zichron Moshe *shul* to *daven* there. Zichron Moshe is famous for its constant *minyanim*; another *minyan* starts every time ten men enter the *shul*. Many of the "regulars" that *davened* at Zichron Moshe were poor and hungry, but their *tefillos* clearly reflected their faith and trust in Hashem.

While Binyomin waited for ten men to come together and begin *davening*, an astonishing scene unfolded itself before his eyes. A car pulled up in front of the main entrance, maneuvering with difficulty through the narrow street. A clean-shaven man in an expensive suit emerged and entered the *shul*, carrying a large paper bag in one hand. He looked around for a minute, as if studying the other people who were there, then nodded his head and apparently came to a decision.

The man opened the bag and pulled out a fistful of money. With a small smile, he laid the bills on the closest *shtender*. Then he thrust his hand into the bag again, pulled out a second wad of money, and laid it on the next *shtender* in line.

For a minute or two, the men in the room just watched in stupefied amazement as the clean-shaven man made his way throughout the room, laying wads of bills on *shtenders*, on the window sill, even on the *bimah*. Binyomin blinked and rubbed at his eyes. Was this really happening, or was it just a dream?

The *gabbai* was the first to break out of his trance. He grabbed one man's hand and pushed it towards one pile of money, calling out, "*Nem, nem!* Take, take!" For another long second, nobody moved; then several of the men began to gather the money together, their faces alight with joy and praise to Hashem for this unexpected gift. Binyomin stood in one corner, watching and marvelling at the incredible scene.

When the man had completely emptied the paper bag, he stood in the doorway and watched as the poor *yidden* gathered the money together and put it in their pockets. Binyomin could not take his eyes off this mysterious man whose face reflected his honest pleasure at bringing happiness to so many people. Then, still without saying a word, the man turned and made his way out of the *shul* to his car. He got inside and drove away.

Binyomin gave his head a quick shake and approached the *gabbai*. "Who was that?" he asked with intense curiosity.

The *gabbai* just shrugged. He had never seen the man before; nobody had. Binyomin questioned several others, but he could not find anyone who could even offer a clue to the strange man's identity.

No one ever discovered who their benefactor had been, but they all agreed on one thing: without question, the man had been a messenger sent from Heaven.

5
WORDS OF OUR SAGES

On the Right Foot
■ ■ ■
A Mother's Concern
■ ■ ■
V'imru Amein
■ ■ ■
A Diamond of a Lesson
■ ■ ■
Run, My Child
■ ■ ■
A Favor Returned
■ ■ ■
A Rebbe's Foresight
■ ■ ■
The Right Doctor
■ ■ ■
Speak Softly
■ ■ ■
The Tenth Man
■ ■ ■

5
Words of Our Sages

ON THE RIGHT FOOT

Everyone would readily agree that Jewish law is not a matter to be taken lightly; it is our guide to obeying the will of Hashem. There are certain laws and customs that may appear trivial to our limited, mortal vision, but the Jew must treat all the halachos with equal stringency. While Hashem does not require us to understand His intentions in giving us the mitzvos, there are times when events serve to shed light on certain halachic requirements. The following story, related by R' Reuven Tillim, is a clear illustration of this concept.

At the turn of the twentieth century, the *yeshivah* did not yet exist on American soil. The only source of Jewish education available was the Hebrew day school, where dedicated *rabbanim* often labored to inject a little enthusiasm for the Jewish religion into boys who were more interested in daydreaming, playing baseball and enjoying all the diversions of the "free world."

R' Yochanan Berman* was among the many selfless men who left the comfortable sphere of Jewish life in New York to settle in cities with tiny Jewish populations in an effort to spread Torah and *yiras shamayim*.

R' Yochanan was determined to seize the opportunity to teach his students as much as possible. When the school year started, he soon established a healthy rapport with the boys in his class. They listened respectfully as he outlined the code of Jewish law and explained all the *halachos* that they needed to know.

One day, R' Yochanan began to teach the section of *halachos* that deals with the proper way to put on one's clothing in the morning.

"The right shoe is put on the first, then the left," he told the boys. "There are many instances in the Torah which show that the right is more important than the left."

The students nodded dubiously.

"However," R' Yochanan continued, "we tie the left shoe first. Even though the right side is more important, tying begins on the left. *Tefillin* is our proof of this, as it is tied on the left arm."

R' Yochanan paused and looked around the classroom. The glazed looks on the boys' faces were a clear indication of their lack of comprehension.

"It seems trivial to you, doesn't it?" R' Yochanan asked gently. He shook his head. "I can't emphasize enough that there is no such thing as a trivial *halachah*. All the laws that Hashem gave us are important, even if our human minds can't understand it."

---

*Names are fictitious.

That night, the principal of the day school received an excited phone call from an angry parent.

"What kind of school is this, anyway?" the father sputtered. "I send my son Philip to your school to learn a little about Judaism and his teacher has to waste time telling him to put his right shoe on before his left one! And then he's supposed to tie the left shoe first?! Why do you have teachers telling the kids such nonsense?"

The principal, who didn't know what the man was talking about, tried to calm him down. "Rabbi Berman is a very wise man and an excellent teacher. Your Philip enjoys his class, doesn't he?"

"That's not the point!" Philip's father snapped. "I don't care how much Philip likes the teacher if the teacher is going to go around telling him such ridiculous things. If that's the kind of teachers you hire, I'm pulling my son out of the school and sending him somewhere else where he can get a *real* education!"

"Let's not be hasty," the principal said in a conciliatory tone. "I assure you that I'll investigate the matter thoroughly and review Rabbi Berman's qualifications." He spent several minutes longer mollifying Philip's father, then hung up and called R' Yochanan immediately.

"Look, here, Rabbi Berman. Are you really teaching the kids that they should put their right shoe on first and then tie the left one before the right?"

R' Yochanan was taken aback by the question. "Well, yes, I am. Why, what's wrong?"

The principal scowled at his telephone receiver. "What's wrong is that the parents don't like it. Can't you teach the boys something that makes a little more sense?"

"I'm sorry," R' Yochanan said firmly, "but I can't allow you to say that the *halachos* don't make sense. I didn't make that up; it's *halachah*. Go look it up, if you don't believe me."

Unfortunately, the principal was not particularly committed to Torah values and knew little about the intricacies of *halachah*. "Look, Rabbi Berman. I can't have you upsetting the students' parents like this. If you can't teach something a little more normal, I'm going to have to ask you to leave the school."

This was a heavy blow for R' Yochanan, who had pinned great hopes on his ability to teach the young boys of the community about *Yiddishkeit*. Still, he felt he had no choice; he could not commit himself to avoiding any *halachos* that might "offend" the students' parents. Sadly, he resigned from his position and left the city to find another job.

Philip's father allowed him to complete the year in the Jewish day school, but without any truly religious teachers on the staff, Philip gained little respect for *Yiddishkeit*. He attended a public high school and went on to complete his education in college. By that point, even the most basic concepts of *Yiddishkeit* were long forgotten. His upcoming marriage to a non-Jewish woman was ample testimony of his cut ties with the Jewish religion.

A few weeks before his scheduled marriage, Philip awoke one morning and began to get dressed. Sitting on his bed, he put on his right shoe, then his left. As he began to tie his left shoe, he suddenly realized what he was doing. Shocked, he remained frozen in place, his mind racing wildly.

Why had he put on his shoes in that manner? He pictured himself as a gangly eleven-year-old boy, sitting in Rabbi Berman's class and listening to the teacher explain why the right shoe is put on first and the left shoe is tied first. All those years, he'd been putting on his shoes in just that way!

"And why am I doing it?" he said aloud. "Because I'm a Jew."

Philip remained sitting on his bed for a long, long time, lost in thought. Then he reached for the phone and called his wife-to-be. When she answered the phone, Philip quietly explained that he would not be able to marry her.

"I'm sorry, but I'm a Jew," he said apologetically but firmly. "I can't marry outside my religion."

Philip did not stop there. He started a long chain of phone calls, contacting his old day school principal, other teachers, and several others before he finally managed to obtain the phone number of R' Yochanan Berman. With shaking fingers, he dialled the number and waited for someone to pick up the phone.

"Rabbi Berman? This is Philip. Philip Rosner, your old student. I - I just wanted to tell you . . . I was about to get married to a non-Jewish lady. Today, for some reason, I found myself remembering the laws you taught us, about which shoe to put on first. It reminded me that I'm a Jew, and I've called off the wedding. I'm going to make it my business to learn more about being a Jew and come back to G-d." Philip took a deep breath. "I owe it all to you, Rabbi. Thank you. I'll never forget you."

He waited for some kind of response, but R' Yochanan was speechless, his eyes swimming with unshed tears of emotion. Who would have imagined that a lesson taught so many years before could have such a powerful impact?

"Rabbi?" Philip said hesitantly after several moments. "Are you still there?"

"Yes," R' Yochanan finally managed to say. "And Philip, I must thank you as well. You have helped me realize something that I don't think I ever really understood before: the power and holiness of every single word of our precious Torah."

A MOTHER'S CONCERN

While every mother worries and cares for her children, the yiddishe mamme also concerns herself with her child's spiritual welfare. Jewish women in different countries and of diverse generations have always displayed concern for their children's Torah education. A menahel of a Midwest yeshivah tells a story to illustrate this point.

The chilly wind seemed to blow right through R' Moskowitz's* coat as he walked up the path towards a large, two-story home. It seemed as if the day had lasted for over a week; first a taxing day in class, then the long evening of interviews with the parents of prospective students for the *yeshivah*. R' Moskowitz often found himself assuming the roles of teacher, principal and spiritual leader all at once, as he tried to convince and persuade skeptical parents that a *yeshivah* education would be beneficial for their son. He was glad that this was his last interview of the evening.

As he knocked on the door and awaited a reply, R' Moskowitz felt his spirits rise. This one shouldn't be too difficult, he told himself. Mrs. Gordon had sounded practically in tears when she called him and begged him to accept her son in the *yeshivah*. With such a cooperative attitude, how difficult could this interview be?

Mrs. Gordon opened the door and brightened at the sight of R' Moskowitz standing on her doorstep. "Come in, Rabbi, come in!" she exclaimed. "I'm so glad you were able to come. Can I offer you something hot to drink?"

Mrs. Gordon led the way into the living room. Her son and husband were already seated side by side on a sofa. Mrs.

**All names are fictitious*

Gordon invited R' Moskowitz to sit in a comfortable armchair before settling down herself.

"Go ahead, Rabbi," she urged. "Tell us about the *yeshivah*."

Mother and son both listened attentively as R' Moskowitz described the *yeshivah* and the Torah education that Meir would receive. Mrs. Gordon asked many questions, and Meir himself seemed very interested, but Mr. Gordon sat silently on the sofa without saying a word.

"I think that covers everything," R' Moskowitz said, casting a wary look at Mr. Gordon. "Are we ready to sign an application?"

"Oh, yes," Mrs. Gordon said enthusiastically.

"Just a minute," Mr. Gordon interrupted, frowning.

R' Moskowitz's heart sank. *It was too good to be true*, he thought with resignation.

"No son of mine is going to a *yeshivah* where they don't study Torah the way they did in Europe," Mr. Gordon declared. He leaned forward with a scowl. "What do you know about Torah study in a European-style *yeshivah*?"

R' Moskowitz stared at the man with astonishment. He was used to opposition from parents who thought Torah study was a waste of time, but he'd never come across an objection like this! "It's certainly true that I never actually studied in a *yeshivah* in Europe," he said slowly. "But I did study under R' Aharon Kotler in Lakewood for several years, and I was able to gain a perception of Torah study as it was in Europe."

Mr. Gordon subsided back onto the sofa, but the frown did not leave his face. "Did you ever hear of R' Yosef Tzvi Dushinsky?" he demanded.

R' Moskowitz felt more puzzled than ever. What point was Mr. Gordon trying to make? "Yes, of course," he replied uncertainly. "He was the *rav* of the city of Chust. He made his way to Eretz Yisrael."

Mr. Gordon stared down at his hands, then looked back up and met R' Moskowitz's gaze. "I was a student of R' Dushinsky," he whispered.

For a moment, R' Moskowitz was speechless. Then he gathered himself together. Despite the unconventional circumstances, he was sure he could use this incident to interest Mr. Gordon in his son's education. "Can you tell me something about R' Dushinsky?" he asked.

Mr. Gordon smiled despite himself. "R' Dushinsky was a brilliant *talmid chacham*," he remembered. "After *davening* on Mondays and Thursdays, people came to ask him questions and beg him for advice about their problems. If there were too many people, and it was taking too long, the *rav's* mother would protest. I remember her banging on the door with her cane and shouting, '*Yossel, Yossel, farbreng nisht der tzeit!* Yossel, don't waste your time! *Du vests bleiben a am haaretz!* You will remain unlearned!' For R' Dushinsky's mother, anything that was not Torah learning was a waste of time. If she felt that her son was spending valuable minutes on trivial matters, she never hesitated to let him know."

"That's a fascinating story," R' Moskowitz said as Mr. Gordon paused. "I've never heard it before."

Mr. Gordon nodded. "The part that always amazed me, though, is how the *rav's* mother could say such a thing. R' Dushinsky was a renowned *gaon*, and his mother was worried that he was spending too much time on things other than Torah study!"

R' Moskowitz glanced at Mrs. Gordon, who was listening anxiously, then smiled gently. "I can't promise you that we'll make your Meir into a R' Yosef Tzvi Dushinsky," he told Mr. Gordon, "but I can tell you that our *yeshivah* turns out boys whose entire ambition for life is to become Torah scholars."

Mr. Gordon smiled, too. "Let's sign the application," he said.

■ ■ ■

Meir remained in *yeshivah* throughout high school. He was a good, diligent student who excelled in his studies. R' Moskowitz provided the boy with support and encouragement during the years and remained in close contact with the Gordons.

At Meir's graduation, Mrs. Gordon stood and watched with tears streaming down her cheeks. R' Moskowitz's *rebbetzin* approached her and sympathetically asked her why she was crying.

Mrs. Gordon wiped her eyes with a handkerchief and explained. "When my son was born, I wanted him to have a *bris*, but there was no *mohel* to be found in the area. We finally located an elderly man who had been a *mohel* in his youth, and we begged him to perform the *bris* on our son. At first, he was very reluctant. He kept saying that he had already retired and was no longer a *mohel*. Finally, when he saw how much it meant to me, he relented and agreed to do the *bris*, but only on one condition: I had to promise that I would make sure that Meir would have a continuing Torah education."

Mrs. Gordon wiped at her eyes again. "All these years, I was never sure that my son would be able to continue learning Torah, as I'd promised. But now that he is graduating from the *yeshivah* and plans to continue his studies in the *beis medrash*, I know that the promise we made to the *mohel* so long ago is truly fulfilled."

She smiled tremulously. "You see, Rebbetzin, these tears are tears of happiness."

V'IMRU AMEIN

Fundamental halachos often tend to be overlooked. In the following story, true faith and courage were instrumental in impressing upon others the importance of a mitzvah.

In the early 1960's, sixteen-year-old Meshullam Yehudah Gross left his home in America and traveled to Europe to further his Torah studies. He learned under a distinguished Rebbe and spent his days absorbed in Torah.

Meshullam often *davened* in the local *shul*. With time, Meshullam became acquainted with many of the other members of the *shul*, both those that were learned and the ordinary laymen of the city.

Meshullam noticed one particular man, Reb Nassan,* a *talmid chacham* who gave a daily *shiur* to the *baalei batim*. Although the man was learned and was able to give beautiful discourses in Torah, Meshullam was troubled to see that Reb Nassan paid no attention to the *halachos* of *tefillah*. Instead of answering *"Amein"* and *"Y'hei Shmei Rabbah"* during the *chazaras hashatz*, Reb Nassan would chat with his neighbor and ignore the *davening* entirely.

Meshullam was highly disturbed by this. How could a man like Reb Nassan, a true *talmid chacham* who devoted his

---

*Name is fictitious

days to educating others, ignore such a clear-cut *halachah*? How could Reb Nassan be so proficient in one aspect of his *avodas Hashem* and so lacking in another?

Perhaps, Meshullam reasoned, Reb Nassan really isn't aware that it is forbidden to talk during *davening*. The law is clearly stated in the *Shulchan Aruch*, but perhaps Reb Nassan was genuinely unacquainted with that *halachah*. Although Meshullam was by nature a modest and unassuming boy, he made up his mind to quietly approach Reb Nassan and point out the error of his ways.

The following morning, after watching Reb Nassan talk continuously during the *davening*, Meshullam approached the older man with an open *Shulchan Aruch*. "Excuse me," he began softly. "I know you are a great *talmid chacham*. I have watched you giving your *shiur*."

Reb Nassan raised his eyebrows at the open *Shulchan Aruch*. "Yes?" He probably thought Meshullam wanted to ask him a question about a certain topic.

Meshullam held out the *sefer*. "I would like to bring a certain *halachah* to your attention. A man of your stature would not transgress the *halachah*, so I am sure you are unaware that one is forbidden to talk during *davening*. Instead, it is of utmost importance to answer '*Amein*' to all the *tefillos*."

Reb Nassan stared at Meshullam for a long moment. "You are a *mechutzaf*," he said shortly, then turned on his heel and walked away.

Meshullam closed the *Shulchan Aruch*, kissed it, and laid it on its shelf. He walked out of *shul* with his thoughts churning wildly. Obviously, Reb Nassan was aware of the prohibition of talking during *tefillah*. His failure to comply with *halachah* was nothing more than arrogance. How could Meshullam convince him of the error of his ways?

That afternoon, during *Minchah*, Meshullam was again disturbed to see that Reb Nassan completely ignored the *chazzan* and spent all his time talking to those around him. As Reb Nassan was ready to leave the *shul*, Meshullam approached him again.

"I am sorry," he said politely but firmly, "but I must speak to you. How can you talk during *davening*? What about the *Shulchan Aruch*? Are you aware of the terrible punishments that await a person who speaks during *Kaddish*?"

Reb Nassan glared at Meshullam. "Who are you to tell me these things?" he demanded angrily. His voice was so loud that many people nearby turned to see what was causing the commotion. "Get away from me before I slap you across the face!" He pushed his way past Meshullam and strode out of *shul*.

The sixteen-year-old boy was undeterred. The following morning, he confronted Reb Nassan once more. "I don't understand how a *talmid chacham* like you can ignore a clear-cut *halachah* in the *Shulchan Aruch*," Meshullam began.

This time, Reb Nassan did not let him finish. In front of all the other members of the *shul*, Reb Nassan's hand flashed out and slapped Meshullam squarely across the face. Many people gasped, but Reb Nassan ignored everyone else and simply walked away.

After the *davening* that morning, Meshullam's *rebbe* called him over to one side. "*Ashrei chelkecha*," the *rebbe* told him with a smile. "Praiseworthy is your portion for giving Reb Nassan *mussar*. I have been greatly pained by this laxity for a long time. I myself have spoken to him, but without success. You will have great merit for your efforts."

Meshullam felt a great sense of comfort at his *rebbe's* words. His humiliation melted away at the knowledge that he had done the right thing.

"I have a *sefer* I would like to show you," the Rebbe continued. "It is called *V'imru Amein*. Learn it and you will see that you have truly accomplished a great deal with your admonishment, even if Reb Nassan refuses to see the error of his ways."

Meshullam accepted the *sefer* and studied it long into the night. The *sefer* put such strong emphasis on the prohibition against speaking during the *tefillos* that he felt even more disturbed than before. If the *halachah* was so stringent, then Reb Nassan surely needed to correct his habits and learn to answer *Amein*!

The next day, Meshullam approached Reb Nassan once more. "I know you slapped me yesterday," he said evenly. "I know you can slap me again. But that won't stop me from telling you that a fine *talmid chacham* like you must obey the *Shulchan Aruch*."

Reb Nassan glared at him. "Get away from me!" he said, his voice rising in pitch until it was close to a shout. "Leave me alone, or I'll throw you out of *shul* myself!"

"That won't change anything," Meshullam replied calmly. "Throw me out of *shul* if you wish, but I will continue to give you *mussar* for speaking during the *tefillos*."

Reb Nassan clenched his fists and scowled at the young boy. "I said to leave me alone!" he yelled before he turned around and marched to the other end of the *shul*. He did not look around as he sat down. Perhaps he was uncomfortably aware that almost everyone was watching him.

This went on for several more days. With each succeeding day, Reb Nassan grew more and more uneasy and self-conscious. Finally, after nearly a week, Meshullam approached the older man to politely remind him once again of the prohibition against talking during *davening*. Before he could say a word, however, Reb Nassan suddenly threw up his hands and shouted, "Okay! I give up! I won't talk anymore."

Reb Nassan was as good as his word. From then on, he no longer spoke during the *tefillos*. Meshullam had saved him from the horrible punishments reserved for those who show blatant disrespect for *tefillah*.

Meshullam eventually returned to the United States and was married. He dedicated himself to enlightening the general public of the importance of answering *"Amein"* and *"Y'hei Shmei Rabbah"* as well as the severe prohibition against speaking during *davening*. To this end, he began to republish *sefarim* in this area, particularly the *sefer V'imru Amein*. Before beginning this project, he approached Rav Yoel Teitelbaum, the Satmar Rebbe, and begged him to give him an approbation. The Rebbe smiled and said simply, *"V'imri Amein!"*

Today, Rav Meshullam Yehudah Gross continues to write and publish many pamphlets and *sefarim* that deal with the importance of saying *"Amein"* and the other *halachos* pertinent to *tefillah*. Thanks to his efforts, many *shuls* have posters of his own design that serve as gentle reminders of this crucial *mitzvah*.

One woman gave Rav Gross a generous amount of *tzedakah* to help fund this important cause. The contribution was dedicated to the memory of her late husband. A few days later, the woman called Rav Gross, nearly incoherent with excitement.

"Rebbe, last night I saw my husband in a dream! He thanked me for giving you the *tzedakah* in his name. He said that his place in *shamayim* had become much higher in the *zechus* of this important *mitzvah*, and he told me to continue to support the cause of answering *Amein* during *davening*."

Rav Gross smiled and said warmly, *"V'imru Amein!"*

A DIAMOND OF A LESSON

In the following story, related by Rabbi Chaim Yaakov Davis of London, a childhood lesson makes an everlasting impression.

In 1946, the East End of London was a scene of grinding poverty. Post-war Europe had little resources for a young boy growing up in England. Chaim Yaakov's father struggled daily to put enough food on the table to feed his family, but R' Davis never failed to emphasize the importance of *Yiddishkeit* and Torah.

One day, Chaim Yaakov accompanied his father to *shul* to *daven*. Unlike many other boys his age, Chaim Yaakov remained in his seat throughout *Shacharis* and prayed diligently, scrupulously answering *amein* to the *shaliach tzibur's berachos*.

When *Shacharis* was over, Chaim Yaakov went into the hallway and waited for his father to fold up his *tallis* and take him home. He was surprised when a man tapped him on the shoulder and told him that Mrs. Diamond, who was upstairs in the *ezras nashim*, wanted to speak to him.

Obediently, Chaim Yaakov climbed the stairs to the *ezras nashim*, wondering what Mrs. Diamond wanted. This elderly woman was a highly respected personality in the Jewish community. Although she made a modest living selling assorted nuts in the marketplace, she spent most of her time collecting *tzedakah* for *yeshivah* institutions. She was dedicated to promoting future generations of Torah scholars, particularly in the wake of the Holocaust. "We need them," she would often say. "Torah scholars keep *klal Yisrael* alive."

Chaim Yaakov entered the *ezras nashim* and made his

way to the front, where Mrs. Diamond was sitting in the same chair she always used for *davening* every day. Mrs. Diamond looked up at him and smiled.

"Hold out your hands, my child," she instructed him. "Hold out both your hands together."

Bewildered, Chaim Yaakov did as he was told. Mrs. Diamond kissed her *siddur*, laid it on the table in front of her, then reached into her pocket and took out a double handful of English coins. With a happy look on her face, she poured them into Chaim Yaakov's cupped palms.

Chaim Yaakov was astonished as he watched the stream of coins pouring into his hands. He'd never held so much money before at one time. Confused, he stammered, "I - I don't understand."

Mrs. Diamond smiled at him again. "My child, always remember to answer *amein* during *davening* as beautifully as you did today," she said simply. And with that, she wished him well and sent him on his way.

The coins that Mrs. Diamond gave him are long gone, but Chaim Yaakov was left with a message he would remember for the rest of his life.

Run, My Child

Life does not always move forward smoothly. A person may encounter difficult times—times of stress, upheaval, turmoil or fear. Often, it is only through complete faith in Hashem that a person may come through these situations unscathed.

The following story was related by Rav Chaim Leib Balgley, late rav in Brooklyn and Kew Gardens.

Gittel, a niece of Rav Baruch Ber Lebowitz (1870-1941), was a mere ten years old at the outbreak of World War I. When the war began, it was decided that she should escape from her hometown of Slutzk. But before she left, she went to Rav Yechezkel Abramsky (1886-1976) to ask him for a *berachah*.

"My child, you have my blessing," R' Yechezkel said gently, with tears in his eyes. "But you must realize that you are embarking on a dangerous path. Crossing the border is a very serious offense."

Gittel nodded. "I realize that," she said, "but I am determined to go."

"In that case, I will ask a favor of you. The *rabbanim* are trapped here. I would like to give you my manuscript, *Chazon Yechezkel*. Please deliver it to the Vaad Hayeshivos, where it can be published. I am sure that this great merit will serve as a *shemirah* for you."

R' Yechezkel handed her the pages of his manuscript. Gittel went into the next room and secured it in her clothing.

"*Tzaischem l'shalom*, go in peace," were R' Yechezkel's parting words.

Gittel left Slutzk and began her journey. She ran for hours on end, until the border was visible in the distance. Even from where she was standing, she could see the soldiers and vicious dogs patrolling the border.

Fear crept into her heart. How would she ever get across? For a moment, she considered turning back. But then she remembered the *berachah* she had received from R' Yechezkel, and her trust in Hashem was fortified.

Stealthily, keeping close to the shadows, she crept close

to the border. She was almost across when the dogs began to bark.

Gittel looked around desperately for someplace to hide. She spotted a small pile of hay lying on the ground. It wasn't much of a hiding place at all, but it was better than nothing.

Lying in the hay, scarcely breathing, Gittel could hear the dogs coming closer. In only seconds, they would discover her.

"Please, Hashem, save me!" she prayed.

And miraculously, the dogs retreated.

Gittel silently thanked Hashem for her escape. She stayed where she was for a little while longer, until the crossing was clear, and then she made it safely across the border.

Gittel arrived in Vilna without any further incident. As soon as she came, she delivered R' Yechezkel's manuscript to the Vaad Hayeshivos.

Years later, after Gittel had married R' Chaim Leib Balgley, the two of them paid a visit to R' Yechezkel in Yerushalayim.

R' Yechezkel waved at the volumes of his manuscript, *Chazon Yechezkel*, which were on the bookcase behind him.

"You see all these volumes?" he said to her. "This is what you saved for me. And it is in *your* merit that Torah students learn from these *sefarim*."

A FAVOR RETURNED

Hashem rules the world with a policy of midah keneged midah—measure for measure. Our deeds and misdeeds are measured on a hairline scale, and we are repaid in kind. To the untrained eye, this is not always evident in everyday life. But those trained in Torah and mussar will see it more readily.

The following incident is related by Rabbi Michael Bender of Stamford, Connecticut.

R' Michoel grew up in the Williamsburg section of New York, where he was surrounded by observant neighbors, *batei midrash*, schools and *yeshivos*, all contributing to a *yiddishe* atmosphere. But most fortunate of all was his family's proximity to Rebbetzin Levovitz, the widow of the famed *mashgiach* of the Mirrer Yeshivah, R' Yerucham Levovitz.

Rebbetzin Levovitz was a powerhouse of Torah wisdom, common sense, and *yiras shamayim*. She often repeated the maxim, "When one does a *chessed*, Hashem sends him a *chessed* in return."

One year, shortly before *Pesach*, Rebbetzin Levovitz came to R' Michoel's house to borrow some *Pesachdik* salt and sugar.

The house was in its usual pre-*Pesach* turmoil. The furniture had been moved to the center of the room and covered with a dropcloth, while the painter finished applying a new coat of paint to the walls.

Mrs. Bender came apologetically to the door. "I'm so sorry, Rebbetzin, but I haven't done my *Pesach* shopping yet, and I don't have any salt and sugar left over from last *Pesach*."

"Mrs. Bender," the painter called. "Do you want me to paint these shelves?"

"Oh, dear!" Mrs. Bender looked flustered. "Those shelves really do need painting, but I have all my *Pesach* items on them, and I have nowhere to put them in the meantime."

"Why don't you put them in my house?" Rebbetzin Levovitz suggested. "Everything is already *Pesachdik*, so I have plenty of room for your *Pesach* items."

"Oh, thank you," Mrs. Bender smiled gratefully. "That would be a tremendous help."

As Mrs. Bender began to empty the shelves, she discovered that there was some salt and sugar left over from the previous *Pesach*.

"Here, Rebbetzin Levovitz," she said with a smile, as she delivered her *Pesach* goods to her neighbor's house. "I can lend you the salt and sugar after all."

"You see?" Rebbetzin Levovitz commented. "I did you a *chessed* by taking your dishes, and in return, Hashem gave me the salt and sugar I needed."

A few days later, the Rebbetzin offered to watch the Bender children to give her neighbor some respite. Mrs. Bender gratefully accepted the offer, happy for a few hours to get some work done without anyone underfoot.

A short while later, Mrs. Bender's young daughter came toddling in the door.

"Mommy, doctor," she demanded. "Mommy, doctor!"

Mrs. Bender stared at her in surprise, then raced for the Rebbetzin's apartment. She found the older woman slumped over the couch, unconscious.

Mrs. Bender immediately called for a doctor, who came over and managed to revive the Rebbetzin. He gave her strict instructions to rest.

After the doctor left and Rebbetzin Levovitz was resting comfortably, Mrs. Bender went to call the Rebbetzin's children. She explained to them that their mother was very ill.

"We'll be there immediately!" they all responded.

Within hours, her children had arrived, and they took care of their mother during her illness. Unfortunately, several days later, Rebbetzin Levovitz passed away.

At the funeral, the Bender family bade a tearful farewell to their dear neighbor, friend and teacher. Mrs. Bender couldn't help thinking of the Rebbetzin's oft-repeated maxim: "When one does a *chessed*, Hashem sends him a *chessed* in return." Rebbetzin Levovitz had done her a *chessed* by watching Mrs. Bender's children so she could rest, and in return, Hashem had Rebbetzin Levovitz's children come to her, so she could get the care she needed.

A Rebbe's Foresight

A Torah leader is one who has absorbed the Torah's teachings into his very being, so every action, word and thought is an expression of Hashem's will. The following story, told by Rabbi Moshe Poupka, a Rosh Kollel in Eretz Yisrael and a student of Rav Yaakov Ruderman (1900-1987) in Yeshivas Ner Yisrael, Baltimore, is a case in point.

While R' Moshe was learning in Ner Yisrael, he became good friends with his roommate, Shmuel*. Shmuel was intelligent and thoughtful, and the two of them had many interesting conversations together. As time went on, however, Shmuel seemed to become withdrawn and unhappy.

"What's the matter, Shmuel?" R' Moshe finally asked his friend.

"I just don't know what's wrong," Shmuel sighed.

---

* *Name is fictitious.*

"Come on," R' Moshe persisted. "There must be something bothering you."

Shmuel hesitated for a moment. "Well, I'll tell you," he said finally. "I don't know if I should be saying this, but the truth is that I'm not that happy in the *yeshivah*. I think I would find more fulfillment in the business world."

R' Moshe couldn't believe it. He had always found fulfillment in Torah learning. The *yeshivah* was his life! And he had always thought that his best friend shared his feelings.

Still, it was clear that he had been mistaken. And telling that to Shmuel wouldn't help any. R' Moshe couldn't think of what to say to his friend.

Then it came to him. "Why don't you discuss it with the *rosh yeshivah*?" he suggested. "He'll be able to help you."

Shmuel brightened. "That's a great idea. I'll see if I can talk to him now."

R' Moshe waited impatiently for his friend to return from his discussion with R' Ruderman. When he saw Shmuel coming back, he jumped up to greet him.

Shmuel looked at his friend. "You'll never believe what R' Ruderman told me."

"Well?" R' Moshe asked. He secretly hoped that R' Ruderman had convinced Shmuel to stay in the *yeshivah*.

"When I told him that I thought I would find more fulfillment in the business world, he suggested that I take a job as a *yeshivah* cook. I told him that I wasn't interested in being a cook."

Shmuel paused.

"So, then what happened?" R' Moshe asked impatiently.

"He said that it is far better to be a cook inside the *yeshivah* than to be anything else outside the walls of the *yeshivah*.

"Then he asked me if that affected my decision. When I

told him that it didn't, he said with a smile, 'At least you're honest.'"

Although Shmuel went on to leave *yeshivah*, the words of the *rosh yeshivah* impressed upon R' Moshe the importance of a Torah atmosphere, and reinforced his intentions to continue in his Torah studies.

Years passed. Shmuel became a prominent businessman, and R' Moshe moved to Eretz Yisrael, where he continued his Torah studies.

One day, R' Moshe was called for routine army reserve training. The procedure began with an inaugural ceremony at sundown, with all the reservists standing at position in full uniform. At a signal, flaming Hebrew letters were shot into the sky. The whole ceremony gave a semi-religious impression, which R' Moshe found distasteful.

As the ceremony continued, R' Moshe began to feel more and more uncomfortable. He considered approaching the commander to protest, but he reasoned that in army training, everything is monitored, and anything out-of-line would be severely punished. So he remained in his place.

Several minutes later, R' Moshe noticed a man with a *kippah* leave his position and approach the commander.

"Excuse me, sir," he heard him say. "I'm a religious man, and I don't think it's proper for me to be present at a ceremony like this."

R' Moshe was impressed at the man's courage and *yiras shamayim*, but he was afraid of the commander's reaction. Apparently, though, the commander was equally impressed by the man's sincerity, and he gave him permission to leave.

Afterwards, R' Moshe went over to the man to commend him on his strength of character.

"I felt like doing the same thing," he told him, "but I was just too afraid to say anything."

R' Moshe then asked him his name and occupation.

"My name is Shimon," the man introduced himself, "and I am a cook in the Ponevezher Yeshivah."

R' Moshe was astonished by the man's statement. R' Ruderman's words echoed in his ears: "It is far better to be a cook in a *yeshivah* than to be anything else in the outside world!"

THE RIGHT DOCTOR

The following story was told by Rav Nassan Wachtfogel, Mashgiach of Beth Medrash Govoha, about Rav Yerucham Levovitz, Mashgiach of Mir (1875-1936).

During R' Yerucham's younger years, he lived in the city of Poltava, Russia. Once, he fell prey to a mysterious illness. Days and weeks passed with R' Yerucham still suffering from fever and weakness. He went from one specialist to the next, but they were all baffled by his condition.

One night, R' Yerucham had a dream. The next morning, he asked one of his *talmidim* to call his close friend, R' Bakst, who was a *talmid* of Rav Simcha Zissel Ziv, the Alter of Kelm.

When R' Bakst arrived, R' Yerucham sent everyone else out of the room. After a few minutes, R' Bakst came out of the room, and he left in a hired carriage.

Toward evening, R' Bakst returned with a doctor, who immediately went in to examine R' Yerucham.

Whispers circulated among the *talmidim*. "This doctor will solve the mystery of R' Yerucham's illness!"

"Strange," one *talmid* commented. "He doesn't look like a specialist."

"How will he be able to diagnose the illness that has baffled so many experts?" another talmid wondered.

To their surprise, the doctor was able to diagnose the illness. He prescribed medication, and R' Yerucham quickly recovered.

R' Bakst was also surprised that this man was able to diagnose the illness, and he asked R' Yerucham about it.

"As you know, I dreamed that this doctor would have the key to my illness, which is why I asked you to bring him here," R' Yerucham told R' Bakst. "And why should this be so surprising? After all, this concept is mentioned in the *Gemara* (*Avoda Zara* 55), 'Every illness will be healed by a preordained doctor and a preordained medicine.'"

SPEAK SOFTLY

The Ramban writes in his famous letter to his son, Iggeres Haramban, "Accustom yourself to always speak softly to everyone at all times. That way you will be saved from (the undesirable trait of) anger."

The following story is told by Rav Nassan Wachtfogel, Mashgiach of Beth Medrash Govoha, Lakewood, New Jersey.

In the Yeshivah of Kelm, the students had a *seder* to learn the *Igeress Haramban* before *Mussaf* on *Shabbos* morning. One *Shabbos*, R' Nassan was sitting next to a layman, who was joining in the *seder*.

About halfway through the *seder*, the man leaned over to R' Nassan. "How far are you?"

"I'm about halfway through," R' Nassan replied.

"That far!" the man exclaimed.

"Why? How far are you?" R' Nassan asked.

"I've been learning the *Igeress* for many years, and I still haven't passed the second line: 'Accustom yourself to always speak softly to everyone at all times. That way you will be saved from (the undesirable trait of) anger.'"

After *davening*, R' Nassan went over to a friend of his. "Who was that man who was sitting next to me?" he asked.

"That was R' Shalom*," his friend told him. "He works in the police station. He runs the whole show there. He's in charge of the records, cases, files — you name it, he does it."

"The police station?" R' Nassan said in surprise. "But the police station in Kelm gets all the low-class people. All the drunken peasants and criminals get sent there!"

"That's right. Imagine what goes on there on a typical day: screaming, hollering, complaints, harrassment. Yet R' Shalom does his job calmly and speaks to everyone softly."

It was then that R' Nassan understood that R' Shalom was actually a giant in *mussar*. No wonder he was only up to the second line in the *Igeress* after so many years!

THE TENTH MAN

A pure word that emanates from the mouth can be so powerful that it may cause a person to accept upon himself a completely new lifestyle.

---

* Name is fictitious.

Deportation to Siberia in Communist Russia was often tantamount to a death sentence. The harsh climate, the lack of food and the harsh labor sapped the hapless prisoners of their strength and left them vulnerable to disease and death. Yonason Laufer*, like so many other young Jewish men deported to Siberia during the war, clung to life with a grim determination to outlive his tormentors and somehow return to a normal existence.

The rations Yonason received were hardly enough to keep body and soul together. Yonason's only option was to attempt to obtain food from the "outside." Such purchases were both illegal and dangerous, but Yonason knew that without supplementary food, he would surely die of starvation.

One evening, Yonason arranged to meet a peasant and purchase a bag of flour. He left camp grounds and furtively made his way to the small village where the peasant was awaiting him.

Just as he was about to enter the little village, another Jew approached him. "Please, Reb Yid," the Jew whispered. "We need a tenth man for a *minyan*. Can you help us?"

Startled, Yonason just looked at him for a moment. Seeing Yonason's hesitation, the Jew elaborated. "A man has just died. We need a *minyan*. We have managed to find nine men, but we need a tenth. Won't you please join us?"

Yonason was torn between his conscience and his desperate need for food. He bit his lip and said slowly, "I am truly sorry, Reb Yid. I have an appointment in this village, and I must be on time. I would truly like to help, but I cannot."

The young man turned and hurried away, leaving the

---
* *Name is fictitious.*

older Jew standing there alone. He felt too guilty to look back.

Without further incident, Yonason made his way to the designated location and purchased his bag of flour from the elderly peasant. But just as the money exchanged hands, uniformed men materialized out of the darkness and pounced upon the two of them. They had been caught indulging in "private speculation," one of the most serious crimes in Communist Russia.

As Yonason sat in his dank prison cell that night, he could not help thinking about the Jew who had begged him to join a *minyan*. If he had performed the *mitzvah* of *chesed shel emes* for the man who had died, he would not have been caught and arrested.

"If I survive this," he said aloud to the damp walls of his cell, "I promise that I will always join a *minyan* whenever I am asked."

Yonason suffered through many brutal interrogations before he was released and given the "freedom" to continue the struggle for survival. When the war finally ended, he was among those who were fortunate enough to be able to emigrate to America, where he married and raised a family.

Yonason Laufer never forgot the vow he had made in the small, dark prison cell in Communist Siberia. No matter how inconvenient, he always agreed to join a *minyan* that was in need of a tenth man. Over the decades, Mr. Laufer became well-known for this particular *mitzvah* and was often called by any *shul* or *shtiebel* that needed a tenth man to complete a *minyan*.

One evening, Mr. Laufer was waiting for his daughter to come and drive him, together with other members of the family, to a family *simchah*. Mr. Laufer was already a great-grandfather, but he was still blessed with good health and enjoyed participating in such joyous occasions.

What with one thing and another, it was already quite late when Mr. Laufer's daughter arrived with her husband and children. "I'm sorry, Tatty," she apologized breathlessly. "We just couldn't seem to get out of the house. We have to go right away if we're not going to miss everything."

Mr. Laufer had already put on his coat and was walking toward the door when the phone rang. "Just a minute, Devorah," he said to his daughter as he picked up the receiver. "Hello?"

"Mr. Laufer? I'm so glad you're home. This is Berel Goldberg calling from the *Shaarei Shamayim shul*. We need a tenth man for a *minyan*. Can you come?"

Mr. Laufer covered the receiver with one hand and looked at his family. "They are calling for a *minyan*," he said slowly. He hesitated, then turned back to the phone. "I am sorry," he said awkwardly. "I am on the way to a family *simchah*, and I really can't keep them waiting. Do you think you can find someone else to complete the *minyan*?"

There was a moment of silence on the other end of the line before the man replied, "Don't worry about it, Mr. Laufer. We'll manage. *Mazel tov* and enjoy the *simchah*."

The following evening, Mr. Laufer, who had never suffered from heart problems before, was suddenly struck by a massive heart attack. The family rushed him to the hospital, but it was too late. Nothing could be done to revive him.

The family was devastated. Mr. Laufer's daughter was particularly distressed and haunted by the knowledge that her father had refused to complete a *minyan* only the day before.

Before a year had passed, Mr. Laufer's daughter was able to draw some comfort from the birth of her tenth son, the first grandchild to be named after Mr. Laufer. For her, this new child represented something more: the son named after her father was the tenth boy in the family, the "tenth man" that completed her own personal *minyan*.

Glossary

aleph-beis: the Hebrew alphabet
aliyah: honorary post at the Torah reading
aron: ark
aveiros: sins
baal teshuvah: penitent
bachur: youth
bar-mitzvah: halachic adulthood
Baruch Hashem: Blessed is the Name
beis din: rabbinical court
beis midrash: study hall
berachah: blessing
b'ezras Hashem: with Hashem's help
bimah: pulpit
bitachon: trust
bris: covenant
chasan: bridegroom
chassid: adherent to *chassidus*
chasunah: wedding
chavrusa: study partner
chazzan: cantor
Chol Hamoed: Intermediate Days of the Festivals
Chumash: Book of the Pentateuch
daven: to pray
ezras nashim: women's section
frum: religious
gabbai: beadle
gadol: great one
gadol hador: greatest of the generation
gaon: genius
Gemara: part of the Talmud
hachnassas orchim: welcoming guests
hakaras hatov: gratitude
halachah: Jewish law
Havdalah: concluding ritual of *Shabbos*
kashrus: state of being kosher
kibbud av v'aim: honoring father and mother
kippah: skullcap
klal Yisrael: the Jewish people

kohein: hereditary priest
kollel: Torah study center
kvittel: supplication
levayah: funeral
Maariv: evening prayers
mashgiach: supervisor
mechallel Shabbos: desecration of the *Shabbos*
mesiras nefesh: complete dedication
mikveh: ritual bath
Minchah: afternoon service
minyan: quorum of ten
mitzvah: Torah commandment
mohel: performer of circumcision
Motzei Shabbos: night after the Shabbos
Mussaf: supplementary service
mussar: ethical instruction
nachas: satisfaction
niftar: deceased
Olam Habah: the World to Come
payos: earlocks
petirah: decease
pidyon haben: redemption of the oldest son
posek: *halachic* authority
rav: rabbi
refuah sheleimah: a full recovery
rosh yeshivah: dean
sandek: one who holds the infant during curcumcision
seder: Passover feast
sefer: book
Shacharis: morning prayers
shalom aleichem: peace unto you; greeting
shamayim: heavens
shemirah: protection
shiur: lecture
shtender: lectern
shtetl: small Eastern European village
shtiebel: *chassidic* synagogue
shul: synagogue
Shulchan Aruch: Code of Jewish Law
siddur: prayer book
simchah: rejoicing, celebration
tallis: prayer shawl
talmid: pupil
talmid chacham: Torah scholar
tefillah: prayer
tefillin: phylacteries
Tehillim: Book of Psalms
teshuvah: repentance
tichel: kerchief
tzaddik: righteous person
tzeddakah: charity
tzitzis: fringes
yarmulke: skullcap
yidden: Jews
Yiddishkeit: Jewishness
yiras shamayim: fear of Heaven
yishuv: settlement
Yom Kippur: Day of Atonement
yom tov: festival
zechus: privilege
zemiros: songs